CHILDREN'S ENCYCLOPEDIA OF BIRDS

Claudia Martin

ARCTURUS

ARCTURUS

This edition published in 2019 by Arcturus Publishing Limited
26/27 Bickels Yard, 151–153 Bermondsey Street,
London SE1 3HA

Consultant: Jules Howard
Author and Editor: Claudia Martin
Designer: Amy McSimpson

ISBN: 978-1-78950-600-6
CH007201US
Supplier 42, Date 1119, Print run 8273

Printed in Singapore

CHILDREN'S ENCYCLOPEDIA OF BIRDS

CONTENTS

A World of Birds

From the rare parrots of the rainforest to the common pigeons of cities, birds can be spotted—or heard—nearly everywhere. Some birds are so familiar that we hardly notice their extraordinary adventures and abilities, from their sudden flights from danger to their beautiful songs.

Finding Food

Although some large birds can survive for several days without eating, most birds spend many hours each day hunting for food. While some eat seeds or grass, others eat fish, insects, or snakes. There are as many different methods of finding food as there are diets. One bird swoops on mice, snatching with its claws, while another rests on a branch, reaching for fruit with its long beak.

These Eurasian hoopoes are sharing a spider that one has caught with its sharp beak.

Extra-long toes enable the comb-crested jacana to spread its weight, so it can walk over the lilypads of its wetland habitat.

Suited to their Habitat

The differences between birds can tell us about their habitat. Forest birds often have toes that curl easily around branches, while seabirds may have paddle-like webbed toes for swimming. Desert birds might have sand-colored feathers to blend into their surroundings, while Antarctic birds have super-thick feathers to stay warm.

Laying Eggs

All birds lay eggs, but there are many different methods of keeping the eggs safe and warm until hatching. Most birds build nests with materials they find, from twigs and leaves to mud and pebbles. Others make use of a hole in a tree, a hard-to-reach cliff ledge, or even the nest of another bird.

Although most birds nest alone or in pairs, sociable weavers build giant nests that house up to 100 pairs along with their eggs and chicks.

When he wants to attract a female, the male fluffs out his colorful feathers.

Communication

Whether birds hunt alone or never leave their flock, all birds can communicate with each other. Songs and calls attract a mate, warn of danger, or drive away a rival. Dances or twisting flights are used to attract a mate. Beak touching or feather fluffing could signal friendliness or anger.

The Gouldian finch's four toes close tightly around branches in the woodlands and grasslands of Australia.

Gentoo penguins recognize the calls of their own chicks as they beg for food.

5

What Is a Bird?

Birds live on every continent, in habitats from rainforests to the frozen coasts of Antarctica. Although not all birds can fly, they do all share some characteristics: wings, a covering of feathers, and a toothless beak. Female birds lay eggs with a hard shell.

Feathered Dinosaurs

Over millions of years, birds evolved from theropod dinosaurs. These dinosaurs had light, hollow bones, ran on their back legs, and—like most reptiles—they laid eggs. Slowly, generation by generation, these dinosaurs developed feathers and their front limbs became wings. By 150 million years ago, dino-birds were making short flights. By 125 million years ago, the first true birds had evolved.

This fossil shows *Archaeopteryx*, a dino-bird that lived 150 million years ago. Like a bird, it had feathers and wings, with which it made short flights. Like a dinosaur, it had sharp teeth.

The green-headed tanager is a species that lives in the tropical forest of South America. Although the bird is brightly colored, its blues and greens act as camouflage among the leaves.

The feathers of this tanager's head and neck are turquoise.

Bird Species

There are around 10,000 species of birds. A species, such as king penguins, is a group of living things that look and behave similarly. Scientists arrange species into bigger groups, such as genus, family, order, and class, based on their similarities. The king penguin is in the genus of great penguins, in the order of penguins, in the class of birds. All animals in the same class share the same basic anatomy, or body plan.

The black and green wings have dark blue covert, or covering, feathers.

Bird Anatomy

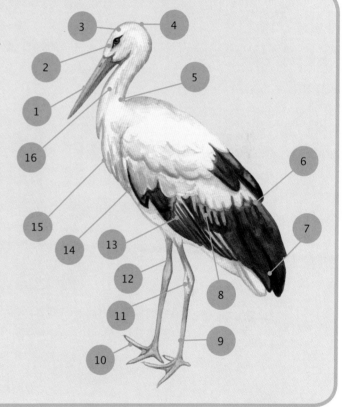

KEY

1. BEAK
2. EYE
3. FOREHEAD
4. CROWN
5. NAPE
6. RUMP
7. TAIL
8. COVERTS
9. UPPER FOOT
10. TOES
11. ANKLE
12. LEG
13. WING
14. FLANK
15. BREAST
16. THROAT

BIRD RECORDS

Biggest bird: Ostrich, up to 346 lb (157 kg), 9.2 ft (2.8 m) tall

Smallest bird: Bee hummingbird, down to 0.07 oz (2 g), 2 in (5 cm) long

Longest-living bird: Pink cockatoo called Cookie, 83 years, in Brookfield Zoo, Illinois, USA

Shortest-living bird: European robins and other small birds: 13 months on average, in the wild

Bee hummingbird

DID YOU KNOW? Most birds have four toes, but a few have three, while ostriches have only two and some chickens have five.

Feathers

Feathers help to keep birds warm and dry. They also play a key part in flight. Feathers are made of a tough material called keratin, which also makes beaks and claws, as well as the scales and hair of other animals.

Feather Types

There are two main types of feathers: contour feathers and down feathers. A contour feather has a stalk, called a rachis, with branches called barbs. Barbs have further branches called barbules, which hook onto the barbules of neighboring barbs, making the feather stiff. Contour feathers form the outer layer of feathers, giving a smooth, streamlined surface. On the wings and tail are longer contour feathers called flight feathers, which help the bird to power through the air. Down feathers do not have barbules, so they are soft and fluffy. They form an inner layer to keep the bird warm.

DOWN FEATHER

CONTOUR FEATHER

BARBS

RACHIS

Preening

Birds need to maintain and waterproof all their feathers, known as their plumage, by preening. They preen using their beaks and claws, positioning ruffled feathers and interlocking barbules that have separated. Most birds also use an oil made in a gland at the base of the tail, spreading it with their beak. The oil creates a waterproof coating.

The common redpoll preens for about an hour a day.

DID YOU KNOW? At least once a year, adult birds molt, slowly losing their old feathers while growing new ones.

FEATHER RECORDS

Most feathers: Tundra swan, around 25,000
Least feathers: Ruby–throated hummingbird, around 940
Longest feathers in a domestic bird: Onagadori chicken, tail feathers of the male, 38 ft (11.3 m)
Longest feathers in a wild bird: Reeve's pheasant, tail feathers of the male, 5.7 ft (1.7 m)
Shortest feathers: Bee hummingbird, down feathers of a newly hatched chick, 0.04 in (1 mm)

Reeve's pheasant

The tail flight feathers, called retrices, help with steering and balance.

The wing flight feathers are called remiges. The largest remiges, called primaries, are farthest from the body and help to propel the bird through the air.

Like other owls, the great grey owl has down feathers on its legs and upper wings to muffle the sound of its flight, so it can hunt silently.

Flight

Birds are able to fly because they are light, with hollow bones, and because of the complex shape and movements of their wings. Different species of birds have evolved different styles of flight to suit their habitat and diet.

How Birds Fly

How can birds stay in the air when gravity always pulls them toward the ground? The answer is in the shape of their wings, which creates a force called lift when they are in the air. Wings have a curved upper surface, so air passing over them has to travel a longer distance than air passing beneath. The faster air above puts less pressure on the wings than the slower air below. This greater upward force keeps a bird in the sky.

Indian rollers get their name from their acrobatic flapping flight. Rollers have short wings with slotted tips.

Balance is important to maintain height and direction. To balance its long neck, the jabiru stork flies with its legs stretched out behind.

Rollers make sudden swooping flights from their tree perches to catch insects, spiders, lizards, and frogs on the ground.

DID YOU KNOW? Bird pee and poop is released through the same opening. Birds expel waste frequently to cut down on excess weight.

Flying Styles

Birds with larger wings can glide through the air, without flapping, held up by the force of lift. Soaring is a type of gliding in which the bird is lifted by rising air. Birds with smaller wings need to do more work to stay in the air: they flap their wings, using their strong breast muscles to power their wings up and down. The angle and movement of the wings creates lift and pushes air to the rear, sending the bird forward, a bit like a swimmer.

Indian rollers live in the forests and fields of southern Asia.

Wing Types

LONG AND NARROW: Gliding and soaring long distances, seen in seabirds such as albatrosses

SHORT WITH SLOTTED TIPS: Acrobatic flapping flight, seen in small forest birds such as sparrows

SHORT AND POINTED: Fast flapping flight, seen in speedy birds such as falcons

BROAD WITH DEEP SLOTS AT TIPS: Soaring on rising air currents, seen in large land birds such as eagles

FLIGHT RECORDS

Longest wings: Wandering albatross, wingspan up to 11.5 ft (3.5 m)

Fastest wingbeats: Ruby-throated hummingbird, up to 200 per second

Fastest horizontal flight: Common swift, 69.3 mph (111.6 km/h)

Longest flight without landing: Common swift, 10 months

Wandering albatrosses

Feeding

Some birds feed on nectar, fruit, or nuts, while others catch insects, small animals, or even other birds. A bird's body is perfectly adapted to its diet and its method of finding food.

Beak Shapes

Studying the shape of a bird's beak can give clues about its diet.

ROSEATE SPOONBILL

DIET: Water creatures such as frogs and small fish

BEAK SHAPE: Long spoon-shaped beak for sifting through mud

OTHER ADAPTATIONS: Featherless head for easy dipping

ULTRAMARINE FLYCATCHER

DIET: Small insects

BEAK SHAPE: Slim, flattened beak for catching insects in flight

OTHER ADAPTATIONS: Fast, acrobatic flight for darting after prey

PIED AVOCET

DIET: Small water creatures such as insects and worms

BEAK SHAPE: Long upturned beak for sweeping back and forth in muddy water

OTHER ADAPTATIONS: Long legs for wading in shallow water

BALD EAGLE

DIET: Fish, birds, and small mammals such as rabbits a and squirrels

BEAK SHAPE: Sharp, hooked beak for ripping flesh

OTHER ADAPTATIONS: Large, curved claws for snatching prey

BLACK-THIGHED GROSBEAK

DIET: Seeds, berries, and insects

BEAK SHAPE: Short, strong beak for opening tough seeds

OTHER ADAPTATIONS: Toe arrangement of three pointing forward and one back, to enable perching on branches

BROWN SKUA

DIET: Fish, birds, eggs, and small mammals

BEAK SHAPE: Long beak with a hooked tip for seizing large prey

OTHER ADAPTATIONS: Strong, large body for attacking and stealing catches from other birds

DID YOU KNOW? Bird tongues, which contain five bones, can be long and sticky for catching insects or spiky for holding onto fish.

The Marico sunbird has a long, downward-curved beak, which it inserts into flowers. Then it uses its brush-tipped tongue to lap up nectar.

At 4.3 in (11 cm) long and weighing just 0.4 oz (11 g), this sunbird can perch on delicate branches.

The male has feathers that are iridescent, or shine in a rainbow of colors.

BIRD DIETS

Omnivorous: All types of food
Piscivorous: Fish
Carnivorous: Meat from any animal
Insectivorous: Insects
Nectivorous: Nectar
Frugivorous: Fruit
Granivorous: Grains and seeds

The common merganser is mostly piscivorous, but will also eat insects, mollusks, and other small water creatures.

Finding a Mate

In cooler regions, birds mate in the spring when the weather is getting warmer. Most species stick with one mate per year. Some species stay with the same mate for several years, while a few, such as cranes, stay together for life.

Colorful Males

In each species, there are usually slightly fewer available females than males, so males must compete with each other to attract a mate. This has led to males often being more brightly colored than females of the same species, with females preferring the brightest. This might be because brightness is a sign of good health, which is a benefit in a mate. Males of some species have evolved other features that are attractive to females, such as long tail feathers.

A pair of male and female red-crowned cranes dance together to create and strengthen their bond, which lasts throughout their lives.

The pair will build a nest, then look after the eggs and chicks together.

The male great frigatebird has a red throat sac that it inflates to attract a female.

DID YOU KNOW? The female northern jacana has very unusual mating behavior: she mates with up to four males each year, leaving them to take care of their eggs.

COURTSHIP GIFTS

Satin bowerbird: Males build females a stick structure called a bower, which they decorate with blue objects

Northern shrike: Males present females with mice or insects stuck on a sharp twig

Gentoo penguin: Males give females a shiny pebble

Northern cardinal: Males feed females with seeds

Great crested grebe: Both males and females offer waterweed

A satin bowerbird with his bower

Dancing cranes bow, then leap into the air with raised wings.

Male blue-footed boobies display their bright feet by lifting them up and down while strutting in front of a female.

Courtship

Males often use courtship to attract a female. A common method is singing, with females of species such as song sparrows preferring males with the widest variety of songs. Males with attractive features, such as the long tails of pheasants, display them by strutting or posing. Some birds, such as male rollers, give acrobatic air displays. Other males build nests to attract a mate, with Eurasian wrens building several nests that will never be used.

Laying Eggs

Female birds lay eggs that must be incubated, or kept at a constant temperature, until they hatch. Most birds lay their eggs in a nest. Some species lay only one egg per year, while others lay several eggs, forming a "clutch."

Nests

It is usually the female that builds the nest, but males of some species help out or take on the job as part of courtship. Different species have their own nest-building style, including cups of sticks and grass; mounds of leaves; shelves of dried spit; and hollows or burrows in the ground. Some birds use existing features, such as holes in trees.

The female sand martin lays four or five eggs in a litter of feathers or straw.

Sand martins nest in tunnels they dig into sandy banks. Up to several hundred pairs nest side by side.

Parenting

During incubation, which takes between 10 and 80 days depending on the species, males and females usually take turns to warm the eggs with their body. After hatching, some chicks are blind, featherless, and helpless. In a few species, chicks are already feathered and able to care for themselves. Females usually care for their young until they fledge (are able to fly) and can defend themselves, while males bring food to the nest. In some species, incubation and chick care is done by one parent alone. Some birds live in groups, called colonies, which share the care of their young.

A female Eurasian coot keeps one of her chicks warm on a floating nest of twigs and leaves.

Male baya weavers begin to build several nests, then court passing females. If a female likes a nest and accepts the male as her mate, he completes the nest.

The nests, which are woven from strips of grasses and palm fronds, take about 18 days to make.

EGG AND NEST RECORDS

Largest clutch: Wood duck and other species, 15 eggs

Smallest clutch: Laysan albatross and other species, 1 egg

Largest egg: Ostrich, 6 in (15 cm) long

Smallest egg: Bee hummingbird, 0.25 in (6.35 mm) long

Largest nest: Bald eagle, 9.5 ft (2.9 m) wide

Smallest nest: Bee hummingbird, 1 in (2.5 cm) wide

A bald eagle nest

DID YOU KNOW? While some birds feed their chicks fresh food, others give food that has been swallowed and regurgitated (brought back up).

Migration

In the spring, flocks of bar–tailed godwits stop over in the Netherlands, on the shores of the Wadden Sea, on the way between their African wintering grounds and their breeding grounds in northern Russia.

Around 4,000 of the 10,000 species of birds migrate every year, moving from one region to another and back again. In cold regions, many birds migrate to warmer regions for the winter. However, even some tropical birds migrate.

Why Birds Migrate

Birds migrate to find food, good nesting locations, or warm weather. Birds that nest in cooler regions find plenty of insects for their young during the long summer days. However, as winter approaches, there is less food, so they may fly nearer the equator or to the opposite hemisphere, where it is summer. In tropical regions, some birds migrate in search of water or to find fruit or nectar.

The barn swallow nests in the northern hemisphere during the spring and summer, then migrates to the southern hemisphere for another summer.

Surviving the Journey

Most birds migrate in a flock, which reduces the risk of any individual being killed by a predator. Birds flying in a flock also have to do less work, as they ride on the air forced upward by the bird in front, called an updraught. Most birds always migrate along the same route, breaking the journey at stopover sites known to have food and water. They find their way using the direction of the sun, by spotting landmarks, and by sensing the Earth's magnetic field, in the same way that a compass finds the direction of north.

Canada geese migrate in a V formation, with the following birds riding the updraught of the birds in front. Birds take turns at being the leader.

18

LONGEST MIGRATIONS

From nesting to wintering grounds and back again

Arctic tern: 50,000 miles (80,000 km), from the Arctic to Antarctica

Sooty shearwater: 40,000 miles (65,000 km), from New Zealand to Russia

Short-tailed shearwater: 27,000 miles (43,000 km), from Australia to Russia

Northern wheatear: 18,500 miles (30,000 km), from northern North America to Africa

Arctic tern

After a nonstop, four-day flight, the godwits double their body weight from 7 oz (200 g) to 14 oz (400 g) during feeding by the Wadden Sea.

The godwits use their long beaks to probe for lugworms in the mudflats.

DID YOU KNOW? The highest migration flight is by bar-headed geese, which can reach 23,920 ft (7,290 m) as they cross the Himalayan Mountains.

Bird Sounds

Birds make two types of voice sounds: songs and calls. Bird songs are long and fairly complex. They often sound musical to human ears. Bird calls are shorter and simpler.

Songs or Calls

Bird song is most common among the passerines, a large order of birds that includes many garden birds. Most singing is done by males, who often sing during courtship. Some sing to defend their territory, battling each other with repeated or changed melodies. Bird calls, made by both males and females, are used as alarms or to stay in touch with other members of the flock.

The laughing kookaburra, which lives in Australia, has a call that sounds like human laughter. It calls to defend the territory of its family group.

Common nightingales are known for their beautiful song, which includes a wide range of notes, trills, and whistles.

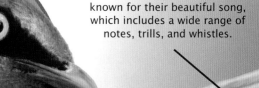

Mimicry

Many bird species, including parrots, mynas, and mockingbirds, are mimics, copying the songs and calls of other birds. When mimics live around humans, they may also copy human speech, ringing phones, or machinery. These birds probably developed the skill as a way to impress during courtship or battles for territory. Imitating the call of a larger bird or predator is also a clever defense.

Like other starlings, the Cape starling mimics the calls of other birds, often adding them into its songs.

DID YOU KNOW? Storks make few sounds apart from clattering their beaks, which they do as an alarm and during courtship.

LOUDEST BIRDS

All heard around 0.6 miles (1 km) away

Eurasian bittern: Low bull-like call of the courting male

Great horned owl: Hooting and shrieking calls of males and females

Kakapo: Booming call of the courting male

Superb lyrebird: Mimicking calls, including chainsaw sounds, of males

Three-wattled bellbird: Honking bell-like territorial call of the male

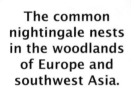

Three-wattled bellbird

The common nightingale nests in the woodlands of Europe and southwest Asia.

Both male and female nightingales sing during the day. If they are looking for a mate, males also sing at night, when most birds are silent. This gave the nightingale its name.

Endangered Birds

Human behavior is threatening 1,200 species of birds with extinction. In the past, humans have driven hundreds of species to extinction, including the Mauritian dodo in 1662 and the North American passenger pigeon in 1914.

Habitat Loss and Damage

When humans cut down forests, expand cities, or use land for industry, birds lose their nesting and feeding grounds. Rising temperatures caused by climate change are also damaging some bird habitats, particularly in the Arctic. Every year, at least 60 million birds are killed by pollution, including the chemicals that farmers use on their fields and leaks from oil tankers. Conservationists are working to protect bird habitats, by creating new laws and setting land aside as national parks.

Only 1,000 Bengal floricans are left alive, because their grassland habitat has been used for farming. The Indian, Cambodian, and Nepalese governments have now created protected areas for the birds.

Hunting

Some birds are hunted by humans for food or feathers, as a sport, or for the pet trade. Today, many countries have passed laws to protect endangered species. Humans have also introduced non-native hunters into some habitats, such as pet cats and rats from visiting ships. These new species, known as invasive species, can prey on birds that have few defenses against them.

Although it is now illegal to trap the Bolivian blue-throated macaw, only 350–400 birds remain in the wild because so many were captured for the pet trade.

DID YOU KNOW? One of the biggest bird killers is collisions: every year, millions die by flying into windows, cars, power lines, and other humanmade structures.

MOST ENDANGERED BIRDS

New Caledonian owlet-nightjar: Up to 50 adult birds, loss of forest habitat due to logging and mining

Kakapo: Around 148 adult birds, hunted by invasive species

Giant ibis: Up to 200 adult birds, loss of marsh and swamp habitat due to farming

Forest owlet: Up to 250 adult birds, loss of forest habitat due to logging and farming

Most kakapo live on two islands off the coast of New Zealand.

By 1987, only 27 California condors were left in the wild, as a result of hunting, habitat loss, and poisoning from lead bullets in the dead animals they ate.

The California condor is a North American scavenger, using its sharp beak to rip into the bodies of dead animals it finds.

In 1987, to save the species, a captive-breeding program was begun: all 27 birds were captured and enabled to mate in the safety of zoos. Today, around 460 condors have been released into the wild or live in captivity.

Birdwatching

Birdwatching is fun in any habitat, from city streets to beaches and woods. A little practice will let you identify many common birds. Even if you cannot name the species, it is exciting to watch and listen as a bird feeds or sings.

Identifying by Sight

When you spot a bird, note its size and body shape. Pay close attention to the beak, which gives clues about diet (see page 12). Note whether the feet are webbed for paddling in water or have claws for catching prey. Look at the plumage color and any bright patches. If you think you can identify the species, check whether it lives in this habitat and region.

Binoculars will enable you to see plumage, beak shapes, and toes more clearly. A notebook and a digital camera that can record sound and video will also be useful.

Guide to Finches

The finches are a family of small, tree-perching birds with cone-shaped beaks for eating seeds. There are dozens of different species, which can be identified by their colorful plumage.

CHAFFINCH

PLUMAGE: Male has blue-gray cap and rust-red underparts

NATIVE TO: Europe, north Africa, and southwest Asia

GREENFINCH

PLUMAGE: Male is green–yellow with bright yellow on wings and tail

NATIVE TO: Europe, north Africa, and southwest Asia

AMERICAN GOLDFINCH

PLUMAGE: Male is bright yellow in summer and olive in winter

NATIVE TO: North America

EUROPEAN GOLDFINCH

PLUMAGE: Male and female have red face and black wings with yellow bar

NATIVE TO: Europe, north Africa, and west Asia

MOST COMMON WILD BIRDS

Red-billed quelea: Up to 1.5 billion birds, Africa

House sparrow: Up to 1.3 billion, all continents except Antarctica

Mourning dove: 475 million, North and South America

American robin: 320 million, North America

Common starling: 310 million, all continents except Antarctica

Flocks of red-billed queleas can destroy crops.

Stay quiet, keep a good distance away from nests, and take any litter away with you, so that you do not disturb the birds and their habitat.

Identifying by Sound

Many birds hide among the leaves, so the best way to identify them is by their song or call. Consider the notes, length, and repeating patterns of any bird sounds, as well as the time of year and day. With an adult's help, match up your findings with the bird calls found in internet libraries.

Red-eyed vireos are small American birds that sing for long periods, with a repeating question-and-answer rhythm.

DID YOU KNOW? Tropical rose-necked parakeets now live wild in southeast England. There are about 32,000 birds, which probably bred from a small escaped flock.

Birds of Prey

Birds of prey are hunters, with strong beaks and claws suited to killing animals that are quite large in comparison to themselves. Many birds of prey are also scavengers, who eat carrion, or the decaying flesh of dead animals.

Beaks and Talons

Birds of prey are in three orders: Accipitriformes, which includes most daytime hunters; Falconiformes, which includes falcons and caracaras; and Strigiformes, which covers the nocturnal hunters—the owls. Although these orders are not closely related, all birds of prey have evolved to have similar beaks and claws. They have a large, curved beak suited to ripping flesh. Their claws, called talons, are long, hooked, and sharp for grabbing prey.

Like all birds of prey, the harpy eagle has talons for seizing and slicing into prey.

Cinereous vulture

LARGEST BIRDS OF PREY

Andean condor: Up to 10.5 ft (3.2 m) wingspan, 33 lb (15 kg) weight—South America

Cinereous vulture: Up to 10.2 ft (3.1 m) wingspan, 31 lb (14 kg) weight—southern Europe and Asia

California condor: Up to 9.8 ft (3 m) wingspan, 31 lb (14 kg) weight—southwestern North America

Lappet-faced vulture: Up to 9.5 ft (2.9 m) wingspan, 30 lb (13.6 kg) weight—Africa and southwestern Asia

Wide-opening jaws enable the secretarybird to swallow prey whole. A strong tongue helps to push food to the back of the mouth.

Unlike most birds of prey, the secretarybird hunts on the ground. It stalks through the grasslands of Africa, then stomps on prey such as lizards, snakes, birds, and mice.

The sharp, hooked beak is used to grasp and strike prey.

Senses

Birds of prey have larger eyes than other birds, giving them excellent eyesight for spotting prey. Their eyes are positioned at the front of their head, more like human eyes than the sideways-facing eyes of other birds. Sideways-facing eyes are useful for seeing predators creeping up, but forward-facing eyes can work together to judge space and distance when chasing prey. Some birds of prey, such as vultures, have a strong sense of smell for sniffing out food, while owls have superb hearing for hunting at night.

Like many owls, the boreal owl has one ear above the other, which helps it work out the height of its prey as well as its distance.

DID YOU KNOW? Birds of prey are also called raptors. Raptor comes from the Latin word "*rapere*," which means "to grab."

Eagles

Eagles are big, powerful birds of prey, with heavy beaks and talons. Most eagles grab live prey from the ground or water surface with their talons, then fly with it to a perch, where they tear it apart. Female eagles are larger than males.

Eagle Eyes

An eagle's eyes weigh about the same as a human's, although its head is far smaller. Yet an eagle can see at least four times farther than a human. This is because its retina, a layer at the back of the eyeball, has 1 million cones per square millimeter (0.002 sq in), compared to 200,000 cones per square millimeter on the human retina. Cones are light-detecting cells that are sensitive to color, so eagles can also detect more colors than humans.

The martial eagle can spot prey as far away as 3–3.7 miles (5–6 km).

Picking Prey

Eagles live on every continent except Antarctica. Depending on their habitat, different groups of eagles feed on different animals. Snake eagles, which live in warm regions, usually prey on reptiles, while harpy eagles feed on sloths and monkeys in tropical forests. The 10 species of sea eagles live along coasts and mainly eat fish and water birds.

On the icy coast of northeastern Russia, Steller's sea eagles fight over a fish.

This bald eagle has plucked a fish from the water, piercing its prey's flesh with an extra-long back talon, while gripping firmly with the three front talons.

The bald eagle is a sea eagle that lives around the coasts, rivers, and lakes of North America.

It has a huge wingspan of up to 7.5 ft (2.3 m).

GOLDEN EAGLE

Length: 26 to 40 in (66 to 102 cm)

Range: Across the northern hemisphere, outside tropical and Arctic regions

Habitat: Mountains, forest, grassland, shrubland, and desert

Diet: Live mammals, birds, reptiles, and fish; carrion

Conservation: Widespread, but disappearing from areas heavily populated by humans

Golden eagle

DID YOU KNOW? If a crowned eagle lays more than one egg, the older chick kills the younger one, either by stealing all the food or by attacking it.

Hawks

True hawks, which include goshawks, sparrowhawks, and sharp-shinned hawks, are small to medium birds of prey. Their long tails and short, rounded wings give them speed and agility as they chase prey, such as small mammals and birds, through their woodland habitat.

Falconry

For thousands of years, human hunters have trained birds of prey to catch birds and other animals for them. Today, this practice continues as a sport, called falconry, often using northern goshawks, Harris hawks, or peregrine falcons (see pages 40–41). The birds are taught to capture prey and then take it to the falconer, earning a reward.

Falconers must use captive-bred birds, such as this northern goshawk, and never hunt endangered species.

Buteo Hawks

Buteo hawks, often called buzzards, are not true hawks. These birds of prey are larger and use their broader, longer wings for soaring rather than swift pursuit. Although buteos nest in trees, like true hawks, they usually hunt over open areas, swooping to capture their prey.

The common buzzard watches out for mammals such as rabbits and field voles as well as snakes, lizards, and insects.

DID YOU KNOW? Hawks, which live alone or in pairs, defend their territories by performing acrobatic looping flights to display their strength.

SHARP-SHINNED HAWK

Length: 9 to 14.5 in (23 to 37 cm)

Range: North, Central, and South America, with northern birds migrating south in winter

Habitat: Woodland and forest

Diet: Small birds

Conservation: Population stable

Sharp-shinned hawk

Standing on top of its prey, a sparrowhawk plucks out the larger feathers before ripping into the flesh.

The male Eurasian sparrowhawk's irises, surrounding the pupil, are orange-red.

Sparrowhawks feed on small woodland birds, waiting on a hidden perch, then flying after prey fast and low to the ground.

Harriers

Harriers are slender-bodied birds with long legs and tails. They make circling flights over open ground as they search for small animals to eat.

On the Hunt

As they hunt, harriers fly low and slowly over grasslands and marshes, holding their wings in a V shape. As well as looking for prey, they listen carefully. Harriers have unusually good hearing for daytime hunters, helped by the bowl-shaped disks of feathers on their face, which collect sounds and direct them toward their ears.

A northern harrier glides over its North American hunting territory.

MONTAGU'S HARRIER

Length: 17 to 18.5 in (43 to 47 cm)

Range: Nests in Europe and western Asia; winters in Africa and India

Habitat: Grassland, shrubland, and wetland

Diet: Small mammals, birds, reptiles, and insects

Conservation: Population shrinking slowly due to habitat loss

A male Montagu's harrier spreads its wings to defend its breeding territory.

DID YOU KNOW? Most birds of prey roost (settle down for sleep) alone or in pairs, but harriers gather in groups at winter roosting sites.

Disks of feathers surround the yellow eyes, giving the harrier's face an owl-like appearance.

Many Mates

Most birds of prey are monogamous, which means that one male mates with one female for at least one breeding season. Some harriers, such as hen harriers, are unusual because they are polygamous, with one male mating with several females, sometimes up to five in a season. The males find food for all the females as they incubate their eggs, then for the chicks after they hatch.

The wing and tail flight feathers are gray.

A female hen harrier feeds one of her chicks in her nest built from sticks.

Kites

These birds of prey have long, pointed wings with which they soar or flap slowly, as well as a long tail for steering them into sudden changes of direction. Kites' slim, light bodies help to make them some of the most graceful flying birds.

Twists and Turns

Birdwatchers love kites because of their acrobatic hunting flights. Kites often soar on rising warm air as they watch for prey, then suddenly dive when they catch sight of insects, small mammals, or carrion below. Some species, including red and black kites, have been known to snatch food from humans who are picnicking.

A red kite swoops toward its prey, swiveling its 70 in/179 cm–wide wings into a twisting dive.

Yellow–billed kite

YELLOW–BILLED KITE

Length: 18.5 to 24 in (47 to 60 cm)

Range: Africa and southwestern Asia, with northern birds migrating south in winter

Habitat: Most habitats, apart from deserts and mountains

Diet: Small live mammals, birds, reptiles, and insects; carrion; human leftovers

Conservation: Not at risk

DID YOU KNOW? For Hindus, the brahminy kite, which lives in southern Asia and Australia, is linked with Garuda, the king of the birds ridden by the god Vishnu.

Like other birds of prey, kites have a waxy structure called a cere at the base of their beak, which contains the nares (nostrils). The black kite's cere is bright yellow.

The black kite's primary flight feathers are black.

Snail Kites

Most kites eat a range of animals, but snail kites usually eat only one thing: snails. These kites, which live in North, Central, and South America, have beaks that are up to 4 cm (1.6 in) long and downward-curved for reaching inside snail shells. Their talons, which they use to pick up snails from the surface of water or plants, are long and slender for tight gripping.

Prey is caught with the sharp talons. If small prey is grabbed in the air, it is moved straight into the mouth without slowing down.

The snail kite usually eats only apple snails. Both the birds and the snails live in wetlands from the southern United States through South America.

Vultures

Vultures are scavengers, usually feeding on dead animals, although they sometimes attack animals weakened by sickness or injury. Vultures live on all continents except Australasia and Antarctica. The American vultures, which include the condors, are not closely related to other vultures.

Scavenging

Most vultures have a bald, featherless head, which stops them getting sticky with blood when reaching into dead bodies. Most species have very strong beaks for ripping into muscles and bones. After gorging on a body, a pouch on the vulture's breast, called a crop, stores food while waiting for room in the stomach.

In southern Europe, North Africa, and Asia, flocks of griffon vultures soar over open land on the lookout for dead or dying animals.

The hooked beak is used for tearing into flesh.

Andean Condor

The Andean condor's 10.5 ft/ 3.2 m-wide wings have a larger surface area than any other bird's. This South American vulture feeds on large dead animals, such as deer and cows. During courtship displays, the bald skin of the male's head and neck inflates and changes color, from dull red to bright yellow. The condor's nest is built from sticks on a rock ledge, as high as 16,000 ft (5,000 m) in the Andes Mountains.

The male Andean condor has folded skin on its neck, forming a wattle, and a fleshy crest, called a comb, on its head.

The hooded vulture has a "hood" of gray down feathers on the back of its head and neck. It lives in Africa, south of the Sahara Desert.

The ear opening is easier to see than in most birds, because it is not covered in feathers.

KING VULTURE

Length: 26 to 32 in (67 to 81 cm)

Range: Central and South America

Habitat: Tropical forest

Diet: Dead or dying mammals, fish, and reptiles

Conservation: Population shrinking slowly due to habitat loss

King vulture

DID YOU KNOW? Vulture stomachs make a powerful acid that kills the bacteria that breed in decaying flesh.

Osprey

The osprey is an unusual bird because it is the only species in its genus and family. Most species share their genus with dozens of similar birds, while families can contain as many as 100 similar genuses. However, the osprey has some unusual features that set it apart.

An Unusual Bird

The osprey feeds almost entirely on fish. Its unusual features are all adaptations that help it catch this slippery prey. The osprey's plumage is thick and its oil gland makes extra waterproofing oil, which helps it stay dry. Its nostrils are closable so they do not fill with water when plunging. The osprey also has sharp spikes on the undersides of its toes that help it keep hold of fish.

The osprey is the only bird of prey, apart from the owls, whose outer front toe is reversible, which means it can grasp fish with two toes in front and two behind.

Light bends as it hits water, making a fish look like it is in a slightly different position. An osprey's eyes and brain are adapted to this, and they are highly accurate hunters.

OSPREY

Length: 20 to 26 in (50 to 66 cm)

Range: Worldwide outside the Arctic and Antarctic, with northern birds migrating south in winter

Habitat: Around coasts, rivers, and lakes

Diet: Usually fish

Conservation: Not at risk in most regions

Osprey

DID YOU KNOW? All birds have a third eyelid, called a nictitating membrane, to protect their eyes. The osprey's is see-through, so it works like goggles underwater.

The primary flight feathers are splayed, making them look a little like fingers.

Eyries

Ospreys build nests, called eyries, on tall rocks or trees. They are also well known for nesting on any high humanmade structure they can find, such as telephone and electricity poles, which sometimes causes fires and power cuts. Ospreys often return to the same nest each season, adding to and tidying the sticks and grass.

This osprey has built its nest on a tower that marks the safe channel through coastal waters.

Ospreys use their talons to grab fish from just beneath the water surface, sometimes plunging right under for a moment.

Falcons and Caracaras

The falconiform birds include falcons, kestrels, and caracaras. They are small to medium-sized daytime hunters with excellent eyesight. Many birds in this group have patterned plumage, often with streaked or striped underparts.

Falcons

Falcons and their close relatives, the kestrels, have a sharp triangular-shaped ridge on their upper beak, called a tomial "tooth," which they can use to kill prey with a swift bite to the neck. With their long, pointed wings, some falcons and kestrels are extremely fast flyers, able to catch other birds in flight. Most will also catch prey on the ground, with forest falcons shaking the branches of trees to flush out their prey.

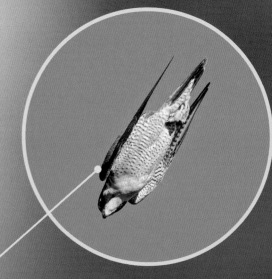

When diving in pursuit of flying birds, the peregrine falcon folds back its tail and wings and tucks in its feet. It strikes its prey with clenched talons, stunning or killing it, then swings back to grab it.

The crested caracara is aggressive enough to drive vultures away from the bodies of dead animals.

Caracaras

Unlike their falcon relatives, caracaras are quite slow in the air. These American birds are often scavengers and are among the few raptors that hunt on foot. Their name is said to come from the sound of the birds' harsh courting and alarm calls.

COMMON KESTREL

Length: 13 to 15 in (32 to 39 cm)

Range: Europe, Asia, and Africa, with northern birds migrating south in winter

Habitat: Grassland, shrubland, and marshes

Diet: Small mammals, such as mice and shrews, birds, and insects

Conservation: Not at risk in most regions

Common kestrel

Each eye has two vision centers, called foveae. The second fovea acts like a telescope and works independently, so falcons see one central image made by the two eyes working together, plus two magnified images of distant prey.

If the peregrine falcon does not kill a bird with a blow from its talons, it uses the tomial tooth to snap its spine.

DID YOU KNOW? The fastest known peregrine falcon dive reached 242 mph (389 km/h), making it the fastest member of the animal kingdom.

True Owls

Owls are the only nocturnal birds of prey. However, a few owls are active at nightfall and dawn, while burrowing owls are active during the day. Apart from during mating season, most owls live alone. Owls species can be found everywhere except the frozen polar regions.

Night Hunters

Owls have several features that help them hunt by night. An owl's huge eyes can pick up a lot of light rays, enabling them to see in almost complete darkness. Sound is particularly important at night. An owl's outer feathers are soft and their wings have a comblike edge, which deadens the sound as they move through the air. An owl can also turn its head through 280 degrees, so it takes "readings" in different positions with its sensitive ears, pinpointing exactly where prey sounds are coming from.

Most owls, such as this barred owl, have plumage that acts as camouflage, mimicking the colors and textures of their habitat. They often go unnoticed during nighttime hunting and daytime roosting.

The eastern screech owl makes a trembling call like a whinnying horse, as well as a purring call on a single note.

Owl Calls

Different owl species make a wide range of calls, including hoots, whistles, growls, hisses, and shrieks, while each species also has different calls for different situations. Owls often call to warn other owls away from their territory, to attract a mate, or to scare away a predator. Some baby owls, called owlets, call to their parents for food.

DID YOU KNOW? Owls swallow small prey whole, but regurgitate the hard parts, such as bones and fur, as lumps called pellets.

Brown facial disks, which are bowl–like arrangements of feathers around the eyes, direct sounds toward the owl's ears.

The spectacled owl preys on any small mammal it can find, from rats and bats to small monkeys such as tamarins.

TAWNY OWL

Length: 14.5 to 18 in (37 to 46 cm)

Range: Europe, western Asia, and North Africa

Habitat: Woodland and forest

Diet: Small mammals, birds, insects, and worms

Conservation: Not at risk

Tawny owl

Barn Owls

The barn owls can be told apart from other owls by their heart-shaped facial disks, formed by feathers that direct sounds to the bird's ears, which are just behind the eyes. While many true owls have earlike tufts of feathers on their head, barn owls never have "ear" tufts.

Super Hunters

A barn owl's facial disk gives it exceptional hearing. It usually hunts by flying slowly on its long, broad wings, hovering over areas where small prey may be hiding. When it hears rustling or squeaking prey, it uses its slender talons to search beneath leaves or snow. When a barn owl catches more food than it needs to eat, it stores extras at the roost to eat later.

The Australian masked owl hunts mammals such as bandicoots and possums, as well as birds, reptiles, and insects.

The greater sooty owl lives in the forests of southeastern Australia and New Guinea, where it roosts in tree hollows, upper branches, or caves during the day.

The head plumage is spotted with white, while the wings are more sparsely spotted.

Barn Owl Parents

Most barn owls stay with one mate for life. Although they may roost alone outside the breeding season, they return together to the same nesting site each year. Barn owls usually nest in a hole in a tree or cliff, or in a rarely used building such as a barn. Females of some species keep their eggs warm by surrounding them with their own regurgitated pellets. Males bring food for the nesting females and later for the owlets.

Common barn owlets are born with a covering of down feathers. By nine weeks old, they are able to fly, but remain with their mother until thirteen weeks while she teaches them how to catch prey.

This owl's call is a falling shriek, often described as sounding like a falling bomb without the explosion.

COMMON BARN OWL

Length: 13 to 15 in (33 to 39 cm)

Range: The Americas south of Canada, Europe, Africa, southern Asia, and Australia

Habitat: Grassland and marshes

Diet: Small mammals, birds, reptiles, amphibians, and insects

Conservation: Population shrinking due to habitat loss

Common barn owl

DID YOU KNOW? The common barn owl's ghostly pale face and screaming call have led to myths that it brings disaster and death.

Water Birds

Some birds live in or around water, finding their food at its surface, beneath the waves, or on beaches and riverbanks. While seabirds live around saltwater seas and oceans, other birds live near freshwater, including rivers, lakes, and marshes.

Adapted to Water

The bodies of water birds are adapted to their habitat and method of finding food. Most water birds make extra preen oil to waterproof their feathers. Birds that swim have webbed feet, in which the toes are joined by skin and tissue, making them paddle-like. Some dive beneath the water to pursue prey, using flipper-like wings. Birds that wade through shallow water have long legs as well as long beaks for probing or stirring. Seabirds that fly far and wide in search of prey have wide wings suited to gliding.

The painted stork hunts for small fish in the shallows of rivers and lakes in southern Asia.

The painted stork puts its half-open beak into the water, then sweeps it from side to side. When the bird feels a fish, it snaps it up.

The common loon uses its large webbed feet to power dives up to 60 m (200 ft) underwater in pursuit of fish and invertebrates.

The dipper has strong, unwebbed claws for gripping the rocks of fast-flowing streams. It dips and dives to grab worms, beetles, and small fish.

DID YOU KNOW? The wandering albatross can fly over 75,000 miles (120,000 km) per year as it watches for fish in the sea below.

Salt Gland

Consuming too much salt is dangerous for birds, just like it is for humans. Seabirds have salt glands in their head to get rid of the salt they take in while drinking and feeding. This means that some seabirds can survive without access to freshwater.

BLACK-BROWED ALBATROSS

SALT GLAND

SALTY LIQUID DRIPS DOWN GROOVE IN BEAK

SALTY LIQUID EXITS THROUGH NOSTRIL

As it wades, the stork uses its large claws to stir up the water and mud, flushing out hiding prey.

DEEPEST DIVERS

Emperor penguin: 1,855 ft (565 m)

King penguin: 1,065 ft (325 m)

Adélie penguin: 790 ft (240 m)

Thick-billed murre: 690 ft (210 m)

Gentoo penguin: 655 ft (200 m)

Common guillemot: 590 ft (180 m)

Thick-billed murre

Waterfowl

Ducks, geese, and swans are all waterfowl. These birds have long, broad bodies, suited to floating at the water surface. They have webbed feet and short, strong legs, set well back on the body for paddling. Their flattened beaks are, in most species, used for feeding on water plants.

Ducks

There are two main types of ducks: dabblers and divers. Dabbling ducks often live around shallow ponds and rivers. They are known for upending: stretching to the water bottom to feed on plants and invertebrates, with their tails in the air. They also skim their beaks across the water surface as they swim. A comb along the beak edges, called a pecten, holds in food but lets water flow out. Diving ducks, which live on freshwater or coastal seas, often dive deep underwater for food.

With his bright plumage, the male mandarin duck looks very different from the brown female. At the end of the breeding season, he will molt into a duller, female-like plumage called eclipse plumage.

A duck's front three toes are connected by webbing, while the shorter, backward-facing fourth toe is unlinked.

Mallard ducks waggle their feet to keep themselves balanced as they upend.

GREYLAG GOOSE

Length: 29 to 36 in (74 to 91 cm)

Range: Nests in Europe and northern Asia; winters in North Africa and southern Asia

Habitat: Lakes, rivers, wetlands, grasslands, and coasts

Diet: Grasses, roots, grains, and fruits

Conservation: Not at risk

Greylag goose

Swans

Swans are the largest of the waterfowl, with the biggest species, the trumpeter swan, having a wingspan of up to 10 ft (3 m). Swans that live in the northern hemisphere have white plumage, while southern hemisphere swans are black and white. Swans' long necks are useful for reaching plants and invertebrates underwater.

A female mute swan gives her chicks, called cygnets, a ride. Unlike most birds, swans lead their cygnets to food, rather than taking food to the nest.

A long tail enables the mandarin to turn quickly as he flies through the forests that surround his preferred East Asian lakes.

Two orange "sails" are formed from extra-large, upturned wing feathers.

Female mandarin duck

DID YOU KNOW? Baby ducks, called ducklings, can swim within a few hours of birth, as long as their mother has spread her own preen oil onto their down feathers.

Cormorants and Snakebirds

Cormorants and their close relatives, the snakebirds, are fish-eaters. They dive underwater from the surface, usually powering themselves with their webbed feet. Unlike other water birds, their plumage is not fully waterproof, so after diving they spread their wings to dry their feathers.

Cormorant Fishing

Cormorants make dives of up to 150 ft (45 m) in coastal seas or in rivers and lakes, capturing fish in their beaks. For hundreds of years, humans have used cormorants to catch fish for them. A thread is tied around the birds' throats, letting them swallow smaller fish but not the larger ones, which are taken by the fishermen. Today, cormorant fishing is still practised in China, Japan, and Greece.

On China's Li River, a traditional fisherman works with great cormorants.

AMERICAN ANHINGA

Length: 30 to 37 in (75 to 95 cm)

Range: The Americas, from the southern United States to Uruguay

Habitat: Swamps, slow-moving rivers, and ponds

Diet: Fish

Conservation: Not at risk

The American anhinga is also known as the snakebird.

A great cormorant dries its plumage. Scientists think its feathers get waterlogged during dives, which has the advantage of making the bird heavier and helping it sink deeper.

The beak is slightly hooked for grasping slippery fish.

The featherless area between the eyes and beak, called the lores, is bright yellow, getting brighter in the mating season.

Snakebirds

Snakebirds, also called anhingas or darters, live in tropical regions. They get their name from their long, thin neck, which they hold above the water as they swim, giving them a snake-like appearance. They capture fish by spearing them with their sharp beaks. When they return to the surface, they toss the fish in the air, then swallow them head first.

Like other snakebirds, the Indian darter has a long, S-shaped neck.

DID YOU KNOW? Cormorants nest in colonies and often hunt together, working as a group to "herd" schools of fish so they can be caught easily.

Kingfishers

Kingfishers are small to medium-sized brightly colored birds that are found worldwide, apart from in polar regions. They have large heads and long, sharp beaks, which are perfect for grabbing fish or insects.

Fishers

Despite their name, only about half of kingfishers specialize in eating fish, which they usually catch in lakes, rivers, and streams. Other kingfishers eat insects, worms, and spiders. Fish-eaters watch for prey from a perch over the water. When a fish is spotted, the kingfisher swoops to snatch it with its beak, dipping into the water. The prey is then smashed against the perch to break its bones.

Found in Indonesia, the cerulean kingfisher seizes fish from streams, canals, and flooded rice fields.

A malachite kingfisher watches for fish and small water-dwelling invertebrates in a pond in Uganda, Africa.

Nesters

Kingfishers nest in holes. Most species dig holes in the earth banks of rivers and lakes. Males and females share the work, starting the hole by flying violently at the chosen spot, then digging with their claws and beaks. The nest itself is in a chamber at the end of a tunnel. Some kingfishers use a hole in a tree or dig into a termite nest, which these ant-like insects have built from earth, spit, and dung.

A brown-winged kingfisher carries a fish to its chicks. It lives along the coasts of Southeast Asia.

DID YOU KNOW? For their riverbank nests, pairs of giant kingfishers dig tunnels up to 28 ft (8.5 m) long.

Although the kingfisher's plumage is gorgeously bright, it is surprisingly well camouflaged when it darts across the rippling blue water.

This kingfisher always returns to its favorite perches, close to the water surface.

COMMON KINGFISHER

Length: 6.3 to 6.7 in (16 to 17 cm)

Range: Europe, southern Asia, and North Africa, with northern birds migrating south in winter

Habitat: Streams, rivers, lakes, and coasts surrounded by bushes or trees

Diet: Small fish and water-dwelling invertebrates

Conservation: Not at risk

Common kingfisher

Flamingos

The six species of flamingos live in tropical regions and the warm regions that border them, called subtropical areas, in the Americas, Africa, Asia, and Europe. Flamingos are waders, feeding in shallow seawater along coasts or in salty inland lakes.

Colony Life

Flamingos live in colonies of up to 100,000 birds. Living together means that birds can keep themselves and their nests safer. In the mating season, males and females break off into smaller groups that dance to each other, stretching their necks and flicking their heads from side to side. When the birds have formed pairs, they build a mound of mud on which to lay their single egg.

A group of flamingos performs a mating display.

Suprising Relatives

Scientists think the flamingos' closest living relatives are the grebes. At first glance, this seems strange, as grebes are swimmers and divers rather than waders, with much shorter legs. However, both flamingos and grebes have 11 primary feathers on each wing, which is very unusual. Similar lice live in the feathers of both groups, which may be because the lice evolved on the ancestors of both flamingos and grebes.

A pair of courting great crested grebes dance to each other, stretching their necks and flicking their heads rather like flamingos.

JAMES'S FLAMINGO

Length: 35 to 36 in (90 to 92 cm)

Range: Andes Mountains of Peru, Chile, Bolivia, and Argentina, in South America

Habitat: Salt and freshwater lakes

Diet: Tiny algae (plant-like living things)

Conservation: At risk from habitat loss

James's flamingo

American flamingos live in Central America, the Caribbean, and northern South America.

Flamingos suck water through their hooked beak, which has comb-like structures along its edges. These hold in bits of food but let water drain away.

Flamingos are pink because of colored substances called carotenoids in the shrimp and plants they eat. Humans get a similar effect from eating too many carrots.

DID YOU KNOW? Flamingo parents feed their young chicks with "crop milk," a goo made by glands in the birds' throat, which they spit up.

Shorebirds

Oystercatchers, plovers, sandpipers, and turnstones are shorebirds that live on beaches and mudflats. They eat small invertebrates in the shallow water or hidden in the sand or mud, often using their sensitive beaks to feel for them.

Opening Shells

The American oystercatcher feeds mostly on shellfish such as oysters, mussels, and clams. It wades through the shallow water where shellfish are firmly attached to rocks and other hard surfaces, looking for one with an open shell. Then it jams in its long, sharp beak, cutting the muscle that closes the shell and eating the soft creature.

If an American oystercatcher finds a loosely attached shell, it carries it ashore and hammers it open with its beak.

Digging in the Sand

Different species of sandpipers have different lengths and shapes of beak, suited to their own method of finding prey: from straight, short bills for pecking at soft sand to long, downward-curved bills for probing deep into mud. Most sandpipers have a collection of touch- and smell-sensitive nerves in a horny swelling at the tip of their beak.

Semipalmated sandpipers probe the sand for invertebrates while wintering on a Florida beach.

DID YOU KNOW? Oystercatchers can drown when an oyster or clam is quick enough to close its shell, trapping their beak.

The crab plover uses its dagger-like beak to pound crab shells, cracking them open.

Like all birds, the crab plover looks as if its legs bend the "wrong" way, but this joint is actually the ankle. The bird's knees are hidden among its feathers.

Partly webbed toes stop the crab plover from sinking into soft sand.

RUDDY TURNSTONE

Length: 8.7 to 9.4 in (22 to 24 cm)

Range: Nests on nothern coasts of North America, Europe, and Asia; winters on warmer coasts worldwide

Habitat: Rocky, sandy, and muddy beaches, and grassland close to shore

Diet: Small invertebrates such as insects and worms

Conservation: Not at risk

The ruddy turnstone flips over a stone in search of tiny invertebrates.

Pelicans and Relatives

The great white pelican is up to 5.9 ft (1.8 m) long.

Pelicans and their relatives, the herons, spoonbills, and ibises, are medium to large water birds with long beaks. They live around sea coasts or at the edges of lakes, rivers, or swamps. Nearly all of them nest in colonies.

Pelican Plans

Pelicans often hunt for fish in groups of up to 20 birds. Most pelicans feed while swimming at the water surface. A group of birds may circle a school of fish, or form a line, driving the fish into the shallows by beating their wings on the water. Each pelican scoops up several fish with its beak, holding them in its throat pouch, which must be drained of water before swallowing. Larger fish are grasped with the tip of the beak, then tossed into the throat. Brown and Peruvian pelicans feed by diving from a height into the water, called plunge diving.

Brown pelicans plunge dive from heights of up to 66 ft (20 m). This image includes several photos, taken within split-seconds.

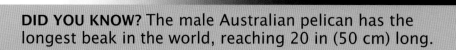
DID YOU KNOW? The male Australian pelican has the longest beak in the world, reaching 20 in (50 cm) long.

SCARLET IBIS

Length: 22 to 25 in (55 to 63 cm)

Range: The Caribbean and tropical South America

Habitat: Coastal mudflats, swamps, shallow lakes, and wetlands

Diet: Insects and small water-dwelling invertebrates such as shrimp and crabs

Conservation: Population shrinking due to habitat loss

Scarlet ibis

Heron Hunts

With their long legs, necks, and beaks, herons are waders. They often hunt by crouching absolutely still at the water's edge, or standing in the shallows. When a heron sees a fish or other small water creature, it moves its head from side to side, working out the prey's exact position in the rippling water by viewing it from different angles. It then seizes the creature with its beak.

The featherless, yellow throat pouch holds up to 3 gallons (11 liters) of fish and water.

The grey heron swallows smaller fish whole, but rips chunks off larger prey.

Pelican parents feed young chicks by regurgitating partly digested food. An older chick can reach into its parent's pouch to eat fresh fish.

Gulls

Gulls are seabirds that nest in large and noisy colonies. Their webbed feet, fairly long legs, broad body, and long wings make them equally good at swimming, walking, and flying. Most of the 55 species of gulls are white or gray, often with black markings.

Adaptable Birds

Gulls are intelligent, bold birds with large, slightly hooked beaks. These characteristics enable them to feed on a wide range of food and to use many methods for getting it. Gulls hunt live prey on water and land, from fish to mice and lizards, as well as picking up eggs, fruit, and seeds. They also scavenge, eating dead animals and human refuse. Some gulls even steal prey from other birds. Laughing gulls are known for grabbing fish from the throat pouches of brown pelicans.

The yellow beak has a dark ring near the tip.

In Sydney, Australia, silver gulls have become so bold they will take food from diners' plates while they are eating.

DID YOU KNOW? When hunting earthworms, herring gulls patter their feet on the ground to mimic the sound of falling rain, bringing worms to the surface for air.

Paired for Life

Gulls usually return to the same mate and nesting colony every year. The biggest colonies have as many as 100,000 pairs and are usually within a short flight of the sea. Most gulls build nests of twigs and leaves on the ground, then lay around three eggs.

A second herring gull chick is using its "egg tooth," a bump at the tip of its beak, to break out of its egg. The egg tooth will fall off after hatching.

The ring-billed gull nests around the coasts, rivers, and lakes of North America, but can be found far from water during winter.

With a wingspan of 4 ft (1.2 m), the ring-billed gull is a strong, acrobatic flyer, often hovering as it watches for food.

GREAT BLACK-BACKED GULL

Length: 25 to 31 in (64 to 79 cm)

Range: Nests on the northern coasts of Europe and North America; roams the North Atlantic Ocean in winter

Habitat: Coasts, wetlands, refuse dumps, and open ocean

Diet: Fish, human refuse, bird chicks and eggs, invertebrates, small mammals, and berries

Conservation: Population growing in number and range

Great black-backed gulls fight over a crab.

Auks

The auk family includes the auklets, puffins, and guillemots. These seabirds look a bit like penguins and have the same hunting technique, using their paddle-like wings to "fly" underwater in search of prey. However, unlike penguins, auks have not lost the ability to fly in the air.

Good Swimmers

Auks have very short wings and tails, webbed feet, and short legs set far back on their rounded body, giving them an upright posture when on land. These characteristics enable auks to float effortlessly on the sea surface, even while they sleep, as well as to dive swiftly when they chase fish and small invertebrates. However, most auks are clumsy walkers. When they fly, auks must flap their wings very fast, up to 400 times per minute, and are slow to change direction.

The Atlantic puffin can catch several small fish in its beak in one dive, holding the first ones with its grooved tongue while it seizes more.

The crested auklet dives in large groups, pursuing tiny invertebrates called krill. During the mating season, birds with bigger crests attract more possible mates.

RAZORBILL

Length: 14.5 to 17 in (37 to 43 cm)

Range: Nests on the northern coasts of Europe and America; roams the Atlantic Ocean in winter

Habitat: Open ocean, cliffs, rocky shores, and islands

Diet: Usually fish

Conservation: Population shrinking due to oil spills and overfishing by humans

The razorbill is also known as the lesser auk.

DID YOU KNOW? Thick-billed murres can hold their breath underwater for 224 seconds: nearly 4 minutes.

Crowded Colonies

Most auks come to land only during the mating season, when they gather in colonies along the coast or on islands. Some species, including crested auklets, nest in colonies as large as 1 million birds. Auks usually lay only one egg, often directly on a cliff ledge or in a rock crevice. Puffins dig a burrow for their egg.

Common guillemots nest in such tight spaces that pairs are touching their neighbors. Birds sometimes preen their neighbors to avoid falling out with them.

During the breeding season, an Atlantic puffin's eyes are ornamented by dark patches of skin above and below, making them seem triangular.

In the spring, adult birds return to the colony where they hatched.

Penguins

All of the 18 species of penguin live in the cooler seas of the southern hemisphere, except for the Galápagos penguin, which lives on the Galápagos Islands, straddling the equator. Adélie, chinstrap, emperor, gentoo, and macaroni penguins spend part of their year on Antarctica.

All at Sea

Penguins' flipper-like wings are so well adapted for swimming and diving that they cannot fly at all. Penguins spend three-quarters of their time in the water, more than any other bird. Although penguins waddle awkwardly on land, their round bodies are streamlined in the water and their webbed feet and wedge-shaped tails are suited to high-speed steering. To keep warm in cool or icy seas, penguins have a thick layer of fat under their down feathers, while their outer feathers overlap tightly, forming a waterproof layer.

Adélie penguins breed on the coasts of Antarctica from October to February, during the southern summer.

At up to 51 in (130 cm) tall, the emperor is the largest of the penguins. It mates on the coasts of Antarctica and hunts in surrounding seas.

The smallest penguin is the little penguin, which is 12–13 in (30–33 cm) tall.

Adélies dive in search of small invertebrates called Antarctic krill, as well as silverfish and squid.

Like all penguins, Adélies have white fronts and dark backs. To underwater predators, such as leopard seals, their white bellies are hard to see against the sparkling water surface. From above, the penguins are camouflaged against the dark water.

Penguin Crèches

Most penguins mate in colonies, with as many as 1 million birds in the case of chinstrap penguins. Emperor and king penguins lay just one egg, which they keep warm on their feet. Other penguins lay two eggs in a nest, either a burrow or a pile of stones. Once chicks are born, the parents take turns at bringing back regurgitated food for them. In many species, once the chicks are a few weeks old they are all left together in a crèche, watched over by a few adults while the parents go hunting.

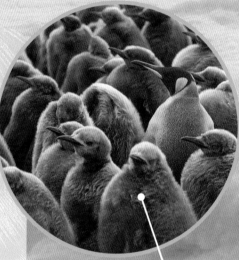

In a king penguin crèche, the down-covered chicks stand close together for warmth in the icy winds of their far-south islands.

ROYAL PENGUIN

Length: 26 to 30 in (65 to 76 cm)

Range: Nests on Macquarie Island in the southern Pacific Ocean; roams in surrounding seas

Habitat: Open ocean, beaches, and pebbly slopes

Diet: Krill, fish, and squid

Conservation: Population reduced by hunting in the 19th and early 20th centuries

Royal penguin

DID YOU KNOW? Gentoos are the fastest-swimming penguins, reaching underwater speeds of up to 22 mph (36 km/h).

Woods, Farms, and Cities

The temperate region is midway between the hot tropics and the freezing poles. This region has four seasons, with cool winters and warm summers. Around half of birds here make a yearly migration. Habitats in this zone include cities, with their parks and yards, grasslands and fields, woods and forests.

Adapting to Humans

Most of Europe, North America, and northern Asia are in the temperate zone, so it is home to a large part of the world's human population. While some birds have become extinct or endangered because of human activity, others live happily in human habitats. City yards offer birds plenty of food and shelter from extreme weather. Many birds, including sparrows and crows, eat farmers' crops, sometimes becoming a pest.

One of the most common passerines in North America, the red-winged blackbird lives in grassland, marshes, and fields.

The American kestrel can be seen perching on city windowledges and signposts as it watches for mice and smaller birds.

The feet are ideal for perching and walking, while the sharp beak is used for grabbing seeds, insects, and berries.

DID YOU KNOW? When a passerine lands on a perch, its toes automatically curl and stiffen, so it can even go to sleep without falling off.

SMALLEST PASSERINES

On each continent

Americas: Short-tailed pygmy tyrant, 2.3 to 2.8 in (6 to 7 cm) long—only some species of hummingbird are smaller
Australasia: Rifleman, 2.8 to 3.1 in (7 to 8 cm) long
Africa: Shelley's oliveback, 3.1 to 3.3 in (8 to 8.5 cm) long
Asia: Pygmy flowerpecker, 3.1 to 3.3 in (8 to 8.5 cm) long
Europe: Goldcrest, 3.3 to 3.7 in (8.5 to 9.5 cm) long
Antarctica: No passerines

The goldcrest is Europe's smallest passerine and its smallest bird.

The male red-winged blackbird, which looks very different from the brown female, has red shoulder patches called epaulets.

Passerines

More than half the world's birds belong to the passerine order. Passerines, also called perching birds, have three toes pointing forward and one backward, which enables them to perch easily on branches, fences, and wires. Passerines tend to be smaller than most other birds and can usually sing well. Many well-known birds are passerines, including crows, tits, wrens, sparrows, robins, and thrushes.

The American yellow warbler is a passerine. It is known for its song, which sounds like: "Sweet sweet sweet, I'm so sweet."

Corvids

The corvids, often known as the crow family, are medium to large passerines. They are very intelligent birds, with large brains compared to their body size. Corvids include crows, jackdaws, jays, magpies, ravens, and rooks.

Clever Corvids

Corvids show their intelligence through their methods of finding food. Pairs of jackdaws sometimes work together: one distracts another bird from its food while the other steals it. Carrion crows sometimes place nuts on road crossings, then wait for cars to drive over and crack them open. New Caledonian crows, American crows, and blue and green jays have all been seen using tools, poking insects out of tree bark with sticks held in their beaks.

The New Caledonian crow is one of the few animals, outside humans and our close relatives, that can use tools.

Magpies and Mirrors

Eurasian magpies have a skill even more unusual than tool use: when they see their own reflection, they recognize themselves rather than thinking it is another bird. It takes human babies until 6 to 24 months old to do the same. In tests, researchers put a colored sticker on the magpies without them noticing, then showed them their reflection: the birds scratched off their sticker.

The Eurasian magpie is very common in Europe and northern Asia.

ROOK

Length: 18 to 18.5 in (45 to 47 cm)

Range: Temperate Europe and Asia; introduced to New Zealand, in Australasia

Habitat: Farmland, grassland, and edges of towns and cities

Diet: Earthworms, insects, grains, fruit, small mammals and birds, and human refuse

Conservation: Not at risk

A young rook

A blue jay raises its crest when angry. This bird is trying to drive a rival away from the nuts and seeds hidden in the log.

Blue jays, which live in eastern North America, have a black collar round their neck.

The primary feathers are boldly striped in black, bright blue, and white.

DID YOU KNOW? The largest passerine is the thick-billed raven of northeastern Africa, which measures 24 to 28 in (60 to 70 cm) long.

Tits

The 64 species of tits are small, round-bodied passerines. They are found in yards, woods, and forests in North America, Europe, Africa, and Asia. In North America, they are sometimes called chickadees or titmice.

Constantly Calling

Tits sing or call almost constantly, only falling silent when avoiding a predator. There are many different calls: from loud alarm calls to a quiet call for staying in contact with other members of the flock while feeding.

Great tits are common visitors at bird feeders in towns and cities across Europe.

The North American chickadees are named after their alarm call, which sounds like "Chick-a-dee-dee." The black-capped chickadee is known for making 13 different types of songs or calls, from gargles to two-note "Fee-bee" calls.

AZURE TIT

Length: 4.7 to 5.5 in (12 to 14 cm)

Range: Eastern Europe and northern and central Asia

Habitat: Woodland, forest, shrubland, and marshes

Diet: Small insects, nuts, and seeds

Conservation: Population shrinking slightly due to habitat loss

Azure tit

DID YOU KNOW? Scientists think that, over the last 50 years, English great tits have evolved to have longer beaks so they can reach into bird feeders.

Great tits prefer to eat insects and spiders in spring, but often eat seeds and nuts in winter.

Flexible about Food

Tits have short, triangular beaks suited to feeding on insects, seeds, and nuts. These birds are good at adapting to the foods available in each season, eating more berries and nuts in winter when insects are scarce. They live happily around humans and often come to bird feeders, where they can be seen in the company of other species of tits.

Eurasian blue tits often feed while hanging acrobatically upside down.

The crested tit feeds on insects, spiders, and seeds, often storing food in tree holes to eat later.

Wrens

These small, usually brown passerines are often hard to spot. However, their loud and complicated songs are a pleasure to hear. Only one species of wren, the Eurasian wren, is found outside the Americas.

The Cave-Dweller

The scientific name for the wren family is Troglodytidae, from the ancient Greek for "cave-dweller." This comes from the habit of some species of creeping into dark crevices to find insects and spiders. The Eurasian wren, the first bird to earn the name *Troglodytes*, also roosts and nests in tree holes and other dark places.

The sharp beak is used to lift leaves and probe in cracks for insects.

The Eurasian wren sleeps and nests in a snug hole lined with sticks, moss, and feathers.

Different Place, Different Song

Wrens are known for their frequent songs, which are sometimes performed by a mating pair as a duet. The house wren lives throughout the Americas, from Canada to Argentina. The songs of all house wrens are streams of bubbling notes, with sudden whirrs. However, the rhythm and the notes are very different in each area, with the home of each bird possible to pinpoint by their song.

The house wren eats insects, spiders, and snails.

SEDGE WREN

Length: 3.9 to 4.7 in (10 to 12 cm)

Range: North and Central America, with more northerly birds migrating south in winter

Habitat: Wet grassland with tall grass or grasslike sedge to nest in

Diet: Insects and spiders

Conservation: Population shrinking due to habitat loss

Sedge wren

The Carolina wren can be identified by its white "eyebrow," a stripe running from its beak, over the eye, to its shoulder.

Wrens usually hold their tails upright, twitching them from side to side as they call or sing.

DID YOU KNOW? Sedge wrens weave up to 20 "dummy" nests from sedge and grass, probably to distract predators from their real nest.

Sparrows

The true sparrows are small brown-and-gray birds with strong, stubby beaks for cracking seeds. They are native to Europe, Africa, and Asia, but some species have been introduced by humans to the Americas and Australasia. Although they share the name "sparrow," the American sparrows are not closely related to true sparrows.

Sociable Sparrows

Most sparrows are very sociable, which means they are often seen in flocks. Outside the mating season, sparrows roost in large flocks in trees and shrubs, with up to 10,000 birds sleeping together. Nesting pairs usually build their nests close together or even share them.

Spanish sparrows feed, roost, nest, and migrate in large flocks.

Dust Bathing

While many birds take baths in water or snow to clean their feathers, sparrows are among the birds that also take dust baths. As a sparrow wriggles around in dry dust or soil, the dust soaks up excess preen oil on the feathers. The oil-soaked dust is then rubbed away, along with dry skin, dirt, and lice.

A house sparrow squirms and flutters as it takes a dust bath.

DID YOU KNOW? The house sparrow was taken to the Americas and Australasia by settlers. It is now one of the world's most widespread and common wild birds.

The russet sparrow is found in the fields, forests, and gardens of eastern Asia.

Although it feeds on the ground on seeds, berries, and insects, this sparrow spends most of its time perching on branches.

The male's head and neck are red–brown. The female has duller plumage.

EURASIAN TREE SPARROW

Length: 4.7 to 5.5 in (12 to 14 cm)

Range: Europe and Asia; introduced to Missouri, in the United States, and southeastern Australia

Habitat: Towns, farmland, grassland, and woodland

Diet: Seeds, grains, and insects

Conservation: Population shrinking in western Europe due to farming chemicals

Eurasian tree sparrow

75

Robins

True robins and bush robins are small, round-bodied passerines found in Europe, Africa, and Asia. They feed on insects and other small invertebrates, flying from a low perch to catch them on the ground. In Australasia and North America, English settlers named similar-looking birds after the European robin.

The European Robin

Known as robin redbreast in Britain, the European robin has an orange breast and face, with brown upperparts and a paler belly. It lives in Europe and western Asia, with birds from the far north migrating to North Africa in winter.

In Britain, the European robin is associated with Christmas, because it is seen hunting for insects, spiders, worms, and berries even when snow is on the ground.

The American Robin

The American robin is actually a thrush (see pages 78–79), but English settlers named this red-breasted bird after the robins they remembered in their fields and yards back home. Unlike European robins, which live alone except when they pair to mate, the American robin roosts in large flocks.

The American robin lives in farmland, woodland, and yards, where it looks for insects and worms when gardeners are mowing lawns or digging.

The orange-flanked bush robin nests in forests in northeastern Europe and northern Asia, but winters in warmer parts of Asia.

The male has a brilliant blue head and upperparts.

This robin usually catches insects on the forest floor.

Golden bush robin

GOLDEN BUSH ROBIN

Length: 5.5 to 5.9 in (14 to 15 cm)

Range: Temperate and mountainous regions of southern and eastern Asia

Habitat: Forests and shrubland

Diet: Mainly insects

Conservation: Not at risk

DID YOU KNOW? European robins will build their nest of leaves and grass in any hole or crevice, including watering cans, bicycle handlebars, barbecues, and hats.

Thrushes

Thrushes are found on every continent except Antarctica. They are small to medium passerines that are usually brown, gray, or black, often with speckled breasts and bellies. They run and hop over the ground as they look for insects, worms, snails, and fruit.

Cup Nests

Most thrushes nest in the branches of trees and shrubs. Their cup-shaped nests are made from grasses, leaves, and twigs, often lined with mud. Females lay up to six eggs in a clutch, with up to three clutches in a year. Parents share the job of bringing worms and other small invertebrates for their chicks. Once chicks can fly, they are often cared for by their father while the mother lays a new clutch.

A male Eurasian blackbird looks after his chicks. Eurasian blackbirds are named for the plumage of the male, but females are brown.

Snail Smasher

The song thrush eats a range of small invertebrates and fruit, but a favorite food is snails. To get at a snail's soft body, it smashes the shell against a stone. It usually returns to its preferred stone again and again.

The song thrush hunts for snails in yards, parks, and woods in Europe, North Africa, Asia, and Australasia.

CLAY-COLORED THRUSH

Length: 9 to 10.6 in (23 to 27 cm)

Range: Southern North America to northern South America

Habitat: Gardens, yards, parks, and woodland

Diet: Earthworms, slugs, insects, and fruit

Conservation: Not at risk

Clay-colored thrush

The fieldfare nests in northern Europe and Asia, migrating further south in winter.

The breast and belly are heavily spotted.

Like other worm-eating birds, the fieldfare finds earthworms by watching for moving earth and listening for faint vibrations.

DID YOU KNOW? Thrushes are very helpful in spreading the seeds of fruit through their droppings, a process called ornithochory (from the Greek for "spread by birds").

Cuckoos

The feet of cuckoos are zygodactyl (from the ancient Greek for "even toed"). This means that two toes point forward and two backward, which is useful for climbing treetrunks. Most cuckoos live in trees, but roadrunners (see pages 106–107) and a few other species live on the ground, where they are good walkers.

Cuckoo Calls

Cuckoos are shy birds that are hard to spot, but their calls can often be heard. Cuckoos get their name from the two-note call of the male common cuckoo, which sounds like "Goo-koo." However, other species of cuckoos make a wide range of calls, from hiccups to whistles.

The yellow-billed cuckoo builds its own nests in the woodlands of North and Central America, migrating to South America in winter.

The male common cuckoo is known for his call, which musicians say is always in the key of C major.

FAN-TAILED CUCKOO

Length: 9.4 to 11 in (24 to 28 cm)

Range: Australasia and the southern islands of Asia

Habitat: Forest, woodland, and yards

Diet: Insects, fruit, and small mammals, reptiles, and birds

Conservation: Not at risk

Fan-tailed cuckoo

DID YOU KNOW? The common cuckoo lays eggs that closely mimic the size and color of the eggs of its host.

Stranger in the Nest

Nearly 60 of the 127 species of cuckoos are brood parasites, which means they lay their eggs in the nests of other bird species, called "host" birds. The cuckoo's egg hatches earlier than the eggs of the host. The cuckoo chick, which grows rapidly, usually pushes the host's eggs or chicks out of the nest.

A common cuckoo chick persaudes a reed warbler to feed it by making begging calls that mimic the sound of a nestful of reed warbler chicks.

The underside of the long tail is patterned in black and white.

The strong legs and zygodactyl feet are suited to creeping along branches on the lookout for insects.

Woodpeckers

Most woodpeckers live in woods and forests, where they use their sharp beak to bore holes in trees to reach insects, which they scoop out with their long tongue. Like cuckoos, woodpeckers have zygodactyl feet for holding onto treetrunks. Woodpeckers are found worldwide, apart from Australasia, Antarctica, and some islands.

Drumming

Although woodpeckers do call, most species also communicate by striking their beaks against a hollow tree, like a stick beating a drum. Each species has a different number of beats in its drumroll. Both males and females drum during courtship and to keep other birds away from their territory.

The drum of a downy woodpecker is a burst of very quick, evenly spaced strikes.

Treetrunk Nests

Woodpeckers nest in holes, which they usually drill into a tree with their beak. It takes about a month to drill the hole, with males doing most of the work. The hole is lined with woodchips. Woodpecker holes are often re-used by other hole-nesting birds.

A European green woodpecker feeds one of its chicks with ants.

DID YOU KNOW? Woodpeckers have skulls of sponge–like bone to stop their brain being rattled about and damaged by pecking on hard wood.

GREAT SPOTTED WOODPECKER

Length: 7.9 to 9.4 in (20 to 24 cm)

Range: Europe, North Africa, and northern and eastern Asia

Habitat: Woodland, parks, and gardens

Diet: Beetles, ants, spiders, bird eggs and chicks, tree sap, seeds, nuts, and berries

Conservation: Population shrinking in some areas due to habitat loss

Great spotted woodpecker

A year-round resident of North American woods and forests, the pileated woodpecker has a bright red crest.

The sharp beak, which is up to 2.4 in (6 cm) long, is used to chip away holes in treetrunks in search of ants' nests.

This bird has found a trail of carpenter ants on a fallen tree. It scoops them up with its long, barbed tongue.

Doves and Pigeons

There are over 300 species of doves and pigeons, which live across the globe, apart from in the icy north and south. There is no agreed-upon difference between a dove and a pigeon. All these birds have plump bodies and short beaks, which are suited to feeding on seeds and fruit.

Domestic Pigeons

Pigeons were domesticated at least 5,000 years ago. Domestication is when an animal is first captured by humans, who breed it carefully so it has useful characteristics. Today's domestic pigeons are descendants of wild rock doves. Some domestic pigeons are racing pigeons or homing pigeons, which can find their way home from up to 1,100 miles (1,800 km) away.

Feeding the pigeons has been banned in London's Trafalgar Square since 2003, because their droppings stain the statues and can spread disease.

Homing pigeons are kept in a house called a dovecote. In the past, homing pigeons were used for carrying messages, which were put in a small tube attached to the leg.

Doves of Peace

White doves and pigeons are seen as symbols of peace and love. They are often released at peace protests and weddings. Doves were linked with peace and love as long ago as 4000 BC in Mesopatamia, in the Middle East, where they were symbols of the great goddess Inanna.

The North American mourning dove is the official symbol of peace of the US states of Michigan and Wisconsin.

NEW ZEALAND PIGEON

Length: 20 to 22 in (50 to 55 cm)

Range: New Zealand, in Australasia

Habitat: Forest, shrubland, parks, and gardens

Diet: Fruit, leaves, buds, and flowers

Conservation: Population at risk from introduced cats and rats

New Zealand pigeon

Many cities are home to feral pigeons, which are domestic pigeons that have returned to the wild.

The birds' wild ancestors roosted and nested on rock ledges, but feral pigeons use any ledge they can find in the city.

DID YOU KNOW? During World War I, the homing pigeon Cher Ami was awarded the French Croix de Guerre medal for carrying a message that saved 194 men.

Tropical Forests

Tropical forests are in the hot region within around 1,500 miles (2,500 km) of the equator. They include rainforest, where lots of rain falls year round; forests where there is a dry season; and montane forests, which are on mountain slopes. More species of birds live in tropical forests than in any other habitat.

Many Species

More than half the world's 10,000 species of birds live in tropical forests. By contrast, only around 250 bird species live in or visit the Arctic and Antarctic. This difference in birdlife is partly because survival is much harder near the poles. In tropical forests, the sun and rain enable plants to thrive. The plants feed plant-eating animals and birds, which in turn feed meat-eating birds.

The hoatzin is the only bird that digests leaves by fermenting them (breaking them down using bacteria) in its crop. This makes a nasty smell, earning the bird the nickname "stinkbird."

The golden monarch is one of 831 bird species found in the tropical forests of the island of New Guinea, in Australasia.

Finding a Niche

In tropical forests, different species of birds often specialize in living in different niches. A niche is a particular region of the forest, from up in the treetops in the canopy, to the trunks and branches of the understory, right down to the forest floor. In each of these niches, a different group of plants and other animals can be found, all of them adapted to each other and the amount of light and water that filters through the leaves above.

The Victoria crowned pigeon searches for fallen fruit on the forest floor in New Guinea.

The hoatzin eats leaves, flowers, and fruit that grow beside rivers and swamps in the tropical forests of South America.

The red-brown crest is long and bristly.

BIRD SPECIES

Countries with the greatest number

Colombia, South America: 1,826

Peru, South America: 1,804

Brazil, South America: 1,753

Indonesia, Southeast Asia: 1,615

Ecuador, South America: 1,588

The turquoise jay lives in montane forests in Colombia, Ecuador, and Peru.

DID YOU KNOW? Up to 60,000 sq miles (160,000 sq km) of tropical forest are cut down every year, putting its birds at greater risk of extinction.

Parrots

The 350 species of true parrots live in tropical and subtropical regions, as well as some temperate regions in the southern hemisphere. True parrots include macaws, parakeets, and lorikeets. Most eat seeds and fruit, but the lorikeets drink nectar.

Parrot Parts

Parrots have a strong hooked beak, with a longer upper mandible (or "jaw"), which is ideal for cracking tough seeds. Their zygodactyl feet have sharp claws, which let them climb tree branches and "handle" seeds and fruit with ease. Most parrots are brightly colored, which is useful for attracting a mate. Among tropical leaves, flowers, and fruits, parrots are surprisingly well camouflaged.

The scarlet macaw lives in the tropical rainforest of Central and South America, where it feeds on seeds, fruit, and nuts.

In most parrot species, males and females look alike, but male eclectus parrots are mostly green while females are red and purple. These parrots live in the rainforests of northern Australia, New Guinea, and nearby islands.

CRIMSON-FRONTED PARAKEET

Length: 11 to 12 in (28 to 30 cm)

Range: Central America

Habitat: Edges of the rainforest

Diet: Fruit, seeds, and flowers

Conservation: Not at risk

Like all parakeets, the crimson-fronted parakeet is a small parrot with a long tail.

Who's a Clever Bird?

Many parrots can mimic human speech and other sounds. This ability has made them popular as pets, which has led to some species becoming endangered in the wild. Among the best talkers is the African grey parrot, which can not only copy words but link some words with their meanings. These parrots can even answer basic questions like "How many blue squares?"

The African grey parrot is endangered. As a result, it is now illegal to sell birds that were captured in the wild.

These macaws often eat salt-rich soil. In their stomach, the soil mixes with and balances out the bitter seeds they feed on.

Macaws are long-tailed parrots that live in the Americas.

DID YOU KNOW? The smallest parrot is the buff-faced pygmy parrot of New Guinea, which reaches only 3.4 in (8.6 cm) long.

Cockatoos

Cockatoos are a family of parrots that live in Australia and the islands to the north, including New Guinea. They have large, moveable crests, which they raise when excited. Cockatoos are less colorful than other parrots, but their crests, cheeks, or tails may be bright.

Family Life

Cockatoos stay with one mate for life, although "divorces" occasionally happen. Pairs preen each other, roost together, and look for food together. Males sometimes feed their mate by regurgitating food into their mouth. They nest in a hole found in a tree, often returning year after year. Some young cockatoos stay with their parents until the next mating season.

Flock Pests

Cockatoos usually live in flocks, calling continuously to each other with harsh shrieks and squawks. Cockatoos eat seeds, grains, fruit, and flowers. When large flocks descend on farmers' fields to feed, they can do great damage to crops, leading to some cockatoos being classified as pests.

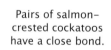

Pairs of salmon-crested cockatoos have a close bond.

The sulphur-crested cockatoo is seen as a pest in parts of Australia because of the harm it does to cereal and fruit crops.

At up to 24 in (60 cm) long, the palm cockatoo is one of the largest cockatoos.

The palm cockatoo uses its tongue to hold a nut against the top mandible of the beak while pressing with the lower mandible to crack it open.

This cockatoo feeds on nuts, seeds, and fruit in woodlands and rainforest in far northern Australia and New Guinea.

A female red-tailed black cockatoo

RED-TAILED BLACK COCKATOO

Length: 20 to 25.5 in (50 to 65 cm)

Range: Australia

Habitat: Rainforest, woodland, grassland, and farmland

Diet: Eucalyptus seeds, grains, fruits, and insects

Conservation: At risk from illegal capture for the pet trade

DID YOU KNOW? While courting, male palm cockatoos drum on a hollow tree with a stick, making a noise that can be heard 330 ft (100 m) away.

Hummingbirds

Ranging in length from the world's tiniest bird, the bee hummingbird at just 2 in (5 cm), to the 9-in (23-cm) giant hummingbird, these are among the smallest birds of all. They live in the Americas, with the greatest number of species in tropical and subtropical regions.

Feeding on Nectar

Although hummingbirds also eat insects, they get most of their energy from drinking nectar, a sweet liquid made inside flowers. They use their long, bendy beaks to reach between the petals to drink. Some species have evolved alongside the particular flowers they feed on, with curved or extra-long beaks to reach in most effectively. Then they lap up the nectar with their long tongue.

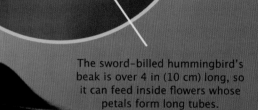

The sword-billed hummingbird's beak is over 4 in (10 cm) long, so it can feed inside flowers whose petals form long tubes.

Humming

Hummingbirds get their name from the rapid beating of their wings, which makes a faint humming noise. Most species flap their wings around 80 times per second. The flapping style and speed of their wings enables hummingbirds to hover in mid-air as they feed from flowers.

The male amethyst woodstar hummingbird (pictured) flaps his wings 80 times per second, while the female flaps 70 times, making a hum on a slightly lower note.

DID YOU KNOW? Hummingbirds fertilize the flowers they feed from by carrying pollen from one flower to the next.

The male marvelous spatuletail has two long, paddle-shaped tail feathers, which he can move independently.

Found only in a small area of Peru, in South America, the marvelous spatuletail is endangered by the loss of its forest home.

As in many hummingbird species, males have a brilliantly colored, iridescent throat. The throat feathers are covered in prism-like cells that split sunlight into a rainbow of colors.

CROWNED WOODNYMPH

Length: 3.3 to 4.5 in (8.5 to 11.5 cm)

Range: Central America and northwestern South America

Habitat: Rainforest, montane forest, and forest clearings

Diet: Nectar, insects, and spiders

Conservation: Population slowly shrinking

A male crowned woodnymph

Birds-of-Paradise

The birds-of-paradise live in the rainforests of eastern Australia, New Guinea, and eastern Indonesia. In many species, males have extremely long and unusually shaped feathers on their tails, wings, or heads, which they use for courtship displays.

Showing Off

Males of most species are polygamous, mating with several females in each season and leaving the females to raise the chicks. These males perform elaborate dances to possible mates, often swinging or ruffling their plumage while hopping on the forest floor or hanging upside down from a perch.

A male twelve-wired bird-of-paradise shows off to a female, displaying his long yellow flank feathers and 12 black, wire-like feathers.

Borrowed Feathers

In Papua New Guinea, the molted head plumes of the King of Saxony bird-of-paradise are collected by male Archbold's bowerbirds, which use them to decorate their courtship bowers (see page 15) to attract females. The feathers are then collected by local people and used in headdresses.

The Wola people of Papua New Guinea use King of Saxony headdresses in their ceremonial dances.

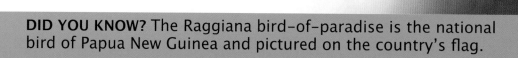

DID YOU KNOW? The Raggiana bird-of-paradise is the national bird of Papua New Guinea and pictured on the country's flag.

A male Raggiana bird-of-paradise performs a courtship dance by clapping his wings, raising his feathers, and lowering his head.

The male has long orange-red flank plumes as well as two long, black tail wires.

Males compete with each other to take the best branches on which to perform.

RED BIRD-OF-PARADISE

Length: 12 to 13 in (30 to 33 cm)

Range: Raja Ampat, in Indonesia, Asia

Habitat: Rainforest

Diet: Fruit and insects

Conservation: Population shrinking due to habitat loss

Red bird-of-paradise

Toucans

Toucans live in trees, where they use their large and colorful beak to reach fruit and birds' eggs while barely moving from their perch. The edges of the beak are jagged for tearing fruit. Toucans are found in the Americas, from Mexico south to Argentina.

Beak Contests

Apart from when they pair off in the mating season, toucans live in small flocks. Their stomachs are quickly filled by the fruit they eat, but it takes a long time to digest, so toucans get time to rest between feeds. They often spend this time battling each other with their beaks, probably so they can establish which birds have greater power in the flock.

Toco toucans fight with their beaks, which are between 6.2 and 9 in (15.8 and 23 cm) long.

Looking for a Hole

Toucans nest in holes or hollows in trees, but their beaks are nearly useless for digging, so they usually find one that has already been made by a woodpecker. When toucan chicks are born, their beaks are short, but grow to nearly full size before they leave the nest, which is after around six weeks.

The red-breasted toucan is known for its croaking and honking calls.

DID YOU KNOW? Despite its large size, a toucan's beak is very light because it is hollow and made only from a bone framework, filled with spongy tissue.

The jagged-edged beak is used for opening fruit and catching insects, lizards, and chicks.

Including its 6-in (15-cm) beak, the keel-billed toucan is up to 22 in (55 cm) long.

Zygodactyl feet are perfect for perching in the rainforest canopy.

COLLARED ARACARI

Length: 15 to 16 in (39 to 41 cm)

Range: Central America and northern South America

Habitat: Rainforest and woodland

Diet: Fruit, insects, lizards, and eggs

Conservation: Population slowly shrinking

Collared aracari

Hornbills

Hornbills live in tropical and subtropical Africa, Asia, and the western islands of the Pacific Ocean. They have long downward-curved beaks, which have a bump, called a casque, on the top. The casque protects and strengthens the beak as a hornbill uses it to grab fruit and small animals.

Balancing the Beak

Unlike toucan beaks, hornbill beaks are heavy. To support the weight, hornbills have extra-strong neck muscles, and two of their small neck bones, called vertebrae, are stuck together for stability. The casque is hardly noticeable in some species, but in others it is large and hollow. It acts like the hollow chamber of a musical instrument, vibrating to make the bird's calls louder.

This hornbill seizes fruit and insects in the rainforests and woodlands of Indonesia, in Southeast Asia.

Looking Ahead

Like birds of prey but unlike most other birds, hornbills' eyes are positioned so they face forward rather than to the sides. This gives hornbills a smaller field of vision, but it means they can see the tip of their beak, so they can position it carefully as they pluck fruit and prey.

Scientists think the bright beak and casque of the male great hornbill help him to attract a mate.

Hornbills have "eyelashes," which are made of adapted feathers rather than hairs. They shelter the eyes from dirt and sunlight.

DID YOU KNOW? While laying eggs, the female knobbed hornbill seals herself inside a tree hole using her own droppings.

The male's casque is high and red. The female's is smaller and yellow.

The male knobbed hornbill has orange-red eyes, which are surrounded by bare blue skin.

RHINOCEROS HORNBILL

Length: 31 to 35 in (80 to 90 cm)

Range: Southeast Asia

Habitat: Rainforest and montane forest

Diet: Mainly fruit, plus insects and small mammals, reptiles, and birds

Conservation: Population shrinking due to habitat loss and hunting

A male rhinoceros hornbill

Trogons

These colorful, long-tailed birds live in tropical forests across the world. They have a unique toe arrangement: toes three and four point forward and toes one and two point backward, which is the opposite way round from zygodactyl feet. The trogon family includes the quetzals of the Americas.

Nibblers

The name "trogon" comes from the ancient Greek for "nibbling," because these birds peck at trees to hollow out nests. Males attract females by singing and calling. All trogons also make frequent calls to defend their territory and raise alarms. Most of the time, trogons sit still on a perch, trying to escape the attention of predators, such as birds of prey.

As in other trogon species, male and female red-headed trogons have different colored plumage. The male has a red head as well as a red breast. Both males and females keep their duller, brown back turned to predators.

Quetzalcoatl

The beauty of the resplendent quetzal (pictured right) led local people to believe it had special powers. For the ancient Maya and Aztec, the resplendent quetzal was linked with Quetzalcoatl, the feathered snake god. Their rulers wore headdresses made of its feathers.

This 16th-century Mexican illustration shows Quetzalcoatl devouring a man.

The green feathers are slightly iridescent, which means they split sunlight into colors ranging from gold to violet.

This quetzal makes only short flights, spending most of its time perched in the forest canopy, where it is well camouflaged.

The male resplendent quetzal has tail feathers up to 26 in (65 cm) long.

COLLARED TROGON

Length: 10 to 11 in (25 to 29 cm)

Range: Central America and northern South America

Habitat: Rainforest, montane forest, and woodland

Diet: Fruit and insects

Conservation: Not at risk

Collared trogon

DID YOU KNOW? Like owls, trogons can turn their heads to look behind them, enabling them to watch out for predators while staying as still as possible.

Estrildids

These small, seed-eating birds are passerines (see page 67). Although some estrildids have the word "finch" in their name, they are not closely related to true finches. Estrildids are found in a range of habitats, from forests to grasslands, in warm regions of Africa, Asia, and Australasia.

Colorful Flocks

Estrildids often feed in flocks, hopping over the ground in search of seeds, insects, and berries. They snap these up with their short, pointed beaks. Although all estrildids have a similar body shape, with a long tail, short legs, and rounded wings, their plumage is in many vivid colors.

Jameson's firefinches (right) and blue waxbills (left) are two species in the estrildid family. They are often seen feeding or drinking together in southern Africa.

Domed Nests

Estrildids build large round or domed nests from grasses, often lining them with feathers. Nests are hidden in long grass, thick shrubs, or thorny branches. As well as using their nests for laying eggs, some species also roost in them at other times of year.

The blue waxbill often makes its nest in an umbrella thorn, right beside a wasp's nest. The wasps may help to keep away predators, but the presence of a wasp's nest also tells the nesting birds that there are no biting ants in that particular bush.

RED-THROATED PARROTFINCH

Length: 4.7 to 5.5 in (12 to 14 cm)

Range: New Caledonia, in Australasia

Habitat: Rainforest, shrubland, and grassland

Diet: Seeds, fruit, and insects

Conservation: Not at risk

Red-throated parrotfinch

The pin-tailed parrotfinch lives in bamboo thickets, rainforests, and rice fields in Southeast Asia.

Like other parrotfinches, this bird has harsh calls, ranging from crackling sounds to clinking noises.

It snaps up seeds and rice in its sharp beak.

DID YOU KNOW? The common waxbill makes an extra nest on top of its main nest, where the parent not currently sitting on the eggs can sleep.

Suboscines

There are two main groups of passerines: the oscines and the suboscines. The suboscines have a simpler structure to their syrinx (the vocal organ of birds) than the oscines. This means that, unlike most passerines, they are not known as songbirds.

A Different Voice

The syrinx is at the lower end of a bird's windpipe. Sounds are made by air flowing through the syrinx and the vibrations or movements of its muscles. Since the muscles in a suboscine's syrinx are much more basic, their voice has a more mechanical sound than those of other passerines.

The manakins are Central and South American suboscines that often make whistling and buzzing sounds. The male long-tailed manakin (pictured) has two very long tail feathers.

Ovenbirds

The eight species of South American hornero ovenbirds get their name from their mud nests, which look like old-fashioned wood-fired ovens. "Hornero" comes from the Spanish word for "oven." It can take several months for a pair of horneros to build their nest, carrying sticky mud from the ground in their beaks.

The rufous hornero usually builds its mud nest in a tree, but may also build in a humanmade structure such as a fence or house.

SPANGLED COTINGA

Length: 6 to 8 in (15 to 20 cm)

Range: Amazon Rainforest, in South America

Habitat: Rainforest

Diet: Fruit and insects

Conservation: Not at risk

The male spangled cotinga does not sing, but makes a whistling noise while flying by vibrating his wing feathers.

This bird makes short whirring or "pauk" calls.

Like most pittas, the female banded pitta is duller on her back, so she is less visible to predators as she searches for small invertebrates on the forest floor.

The Malayan banded pitta lives in Malaysia, Thailand, and Sumatra, in Southeast Asia.

DID YOU KNOW? There are around 5,000 species of oscines but only 1,000 suboscines, most of them living in South America and other tropical regions.

On the Ground

Some birds not only feed on the ground but also roost and nest on it. They are called ground-dwelling, or terrestrial, birds. Some ground-dwellers are completely unable to fly, while others are clumsy flyers, making only short, low flights.

Survival on the Ground

Ground-dwelling birds tend to have plumper bodies and shorter wings than other birds. Yet they usually have longer and stronger legs, enabling them to run fast away from predators, particularly if they cannot fly. When nesting on the ground, females are at risk from predators, so they are often dull colored for camouflage. To give newborn chicks some protection from predators, they are already covered in down feathers and are soon able to walk.

With their brown–orange, speckled plumage, a female and chick Namaqua sandgrouse are well camouflaged against the sand and dry grasses of their African habitat. The chick is resting in its mother's shadow.

FLIGHTLESS BIRD RECORDS

Largest: Common ostrich, up to 344 lb (156 kg), 9.2 ft (2.8 m) tall, making it the biggest bird of all

Smallest: Inaccessible Island rail, 1.2 oz (34 g), 5.1 in (13 cm) long

Fastest runner: Common ostrich, 43 mph (69 km/h), making it the fastest-running bird of all

Longest claws: Southern cassowary, 5 in (12.7 cm) long, making it the longest-clawed bird of all

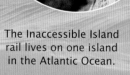

The Inaccessible Island rail lives on one island in the Atlantic Ocean.

DID YOU KNOW? New Zealand's small flightless birds, including the kakapo, weka, takahe, and five species of kiwis, are all at high risk of extinction.

The greater roadrunner lives in shrubland in the southwestern United States and Mexico.

Its long, strong legs make this roadrunner the fastest-running flighted bird, reaching 26 mph (42 km/h) as it chases lizards, insects, spiders, and mice.

When escaping predators such as coyotes, the roadrunner can make brief flights with its short, rounded wings.

Around 20 in (50 cm) long, the North Island brown kiwi is one of 16 species of small flightless birds found on the islands of New Zealand.

Flightless Birds

Around 60 species of birds cannot fly at all. Around half of them are water birds: penguins and flightless ducks, grebes, and cormorants evolved to be good swimmers instead of flyers. The land-dwelling flightless birds evolved to be so successful on the ground that they lost the need for flight. The most well-known group is the ratites, including the emu, cassowaries, ostriches, rheas, and kiwis. Most ratites are very large and excellent runners. However, the kiwis—along with flightless birds in other groups, such as the rails—are quite small. Small flightless birds are found only on islands where, before the arrival of humans, there were no large predators.

Emu and Family

The emu and cassowaries make up the Casuariidae family, in the ratite group of flightless birds. Like other ratites, they have smaller wing bones and weaker wing muscles than flying birds. The emu and cassowaries are very large, with long legs and necks, and three-toed feet with sharp claws.

The Emu

The single species of emu lives across much of Australia, where it eats seeds, leaves, insects, and spiders. It sometimes goes several days without water, when it cannot find a waterhole to drink from. The emu can run at up to 30 mph (50 km/h) to escape predators, flapping its small wings for balance. If cornered by a wild dog or crocodile, it kicks out with its sharp claws.

Emu feathers are soft because the vanes are not held together by barbules. Like other ratites, emus do not have preen glands, as they do not need to smooth their feathers for flight.

The Cassowaries

There are three species of cassowaries: the southern, northern, and dwarf. They all live in tropical forests in New Guinea and nearby islands, while the southern cassowary is also found in northeastern Australia. Cassowaries have a bump, called a casque, on their head, which amplifies their calls. The claw on a cassowary's middle toe is so sharp that a kick can be deadly to predators or humans.

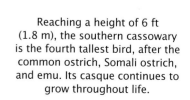

Reaching a height of 6 ft (1.8 m), the southern cassowary is the fourth tallest bird, after the common ostrich, Somali ostrich, and emu. Its casque continues to grow throughout life.

108

NORTHERN CASSOWARY

Length: 3.9 to 4.9 ft (1.2 to 1.5 m); 4.9 to 5.9 ft (1.5 to 1.8 m) tall

Range: New Guinea and nearby, in Australasia

Habitat: Rainforest and swamp forest

Diet: Mainly fruit, plus mice, rats, lizards, frogs, birds, insects, and snails

Conservation: Population slowly shrinking

Northern cassowary

Emus grow up to 6.2 ft (1.9 m) tall, with males slightly shorter than females.

The male emu looks after his chicks for the first seven months. The mother fights other females to find a new mate, then nests again, up to three times in each year.

Young chicks, which are just 5 in (12 cm) tall at birth, are striped for camouflage.

DID YOU KNOW? Emus swallow small stones to grind up the plants they eat, holding the stones in a separate, thick-walled stomach chamber called the gizzard.

Ostriches and Rheas

The lesser rhea lives at heights of up to 14,800 ft (4,500 m) in the Andes Mountains.

These long-necked, long-legged flightless birds belong to the ratite group. The two species of ostriches are found in Africa, while the two rheas live in South America. Many scientists think the ratites evolved when these continents were part of one giant landmass.

Speedy Ostriches

The Somali and common ostriches are the only birds with just two toes on each foot. The inner toe has a large hooflike claw, while the much smaller outer toe has no claw. It is this horse-like foot shape that enables ostriches to be the world's fastest-running birds, able to "jog" at 34 mph (55 km/h) for 30 minutes. Speed is vital, as their predators include cheetahs, lions, and spotted hyenas.

Male ostriches mate with up to seven females, who all lay eggs in one pit. The females incubate the eggs during the day (pictured) because their brown plumage is good camouflage. The male, who has black plumage, incubates at night.

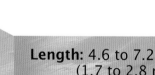

COMMON OSTRICH

Length: 4.6 to 7.2 ft (1.4 to 2.2 m); 5.6 to 9.2 ft (1.7 to 2.8 m) tall

Range: Central, eastern, and southern Africa

Habitat: Dry grassland and shrubland

Diet: Seeds, leaves, grass, fruit, flowers, and insects

Conservation: Population slowly shrinking

The skin of this male common ostrich has flushed pink during mating season.

Zigzaging Rheas

Rheas have unusually large wings for flightless birds. They spread these while running, using them like sails to catch the wind, giving a sudden burst of speed. When fleeing from a predator, such as a cougar or jaguar, rheas often run in a zigzag, first opening one wing then the other.

At up to 5.2 ft (1.6 m) tall, the lesser rhea is a little shorter than the greater rhea.

It feeds on shrubs, cactus fruits, lizards, and insects.

Male greater rheas mate with up to 12 females in each year. When courting females, the male ruffles his plumage and raises his wings.

DID YOU KNOW? Common ostriches have the largest eyes of any land animal, 2 in (5 cm) across, enabling them to see predators far away across the grasslands.

111

Chickens

Chickens are domesticated birds, which means they are kept by humans, either on farms or as pets. Chickens are a type of landfowl, which are plump-bodied birds that can escape predators with short bursts of flight, but spend most of their life on the ground.

Domestication

Chickens are kept for their meat and eggs. They are descended from wild red junglefowl, which were first captured by humans at least 5,000 years ago in Asia. Chickens and red junglefowl belong to the same species, *Gallus gallus*. Since modern chickens look a bit different from red junglefowl, scientists say chickens are a subspecies, naming them *Gallus gallus domesticus*.

Like chickens, male and female red junglefowl look different from each other. The male, called a rooster, has a tail of black, arching feathers and a red comb on his head. The female, called a hen, cares for the eggs and chicks, so is better camouflaged.

MALE

FEMALE

Polish chicken

DOMESTIC CHICKEN

Length: 12 to 34 in (30 to 86 cm)

Range: Worldwide, except Antarctica

Habitat: Farms and gardens

Diet: Grains, grass, fruit, vegetables, insects, slugs, and worms

Conservation: Population growing

DID YOU KNOW? There are around 19 billion chickens in the world, making them the world's most common bird.

Breeds

Over time, humans have bred chickens to have particular characteristics, by pairing parent birds with features that they liked. This has created over 500 different chicken breeds, all still belonging to the same subspecies. Some breeds are kept for their egg-laying ability, while other, "ornamental" breeds have fancy plumage.

All adult chickens have flaps of skin below their beak, called wattles, and a comb on their head, although these features are normally larger in roosters.

A hen guards her chicks closely until they are 8 to 10 weeks old. She will warm them by nestling close to them until they grow their adult feathers.

The silkie ornamental breed has very soft, long plumage. These birds are popular pets because they are calm and friendly.

The chicks are led to food and water by their mother.

Turkeys

There are two species of turkeys, the ocellated turkey, which lives only in the Yucatán Peninsula of Mexico, and the wild turkey, which lives in forests in North America. The domestic turkey, which lives on farms around the world, is the same species as the wild turkey.

Male Displays

Like other male landfowl, male turkeys are bigger and more colorful than females. Males of both turkey species have a long fleshy lump, called a snood, dangling from their forehead. When the male starts his courtship display, the snood fills with blood, becoming darker and longer. At the same time, he puffs out his feathers, fans his tail, and struts.

This male wild turkey's snood is so full of blood that it is flushed scarlet and hanging well below his beak. Females are attracted to males with the longest snoods.

A male ocellated turkey performs a courtship display, while a female looks on.

DID YOU KNOW? In the mating season, male turkeys make a loud, gurgling sound called a "gobble" to attract females, while hens respond with a sharp "yelp" noise.

DOMESTIC TURKEY

Length: 3.3 to 4.1 ft (1 to 1.25 m)

Range: Worldwide, except Antarctica

Habitat: Farms and gardens

Diet: Grains, seeds, nuts, fruit, vegetables, and insects and other invertebrates

Conservation: Population stable

A female of the Norfolk black breed

Small fleshy bumps called caruncles are on the head and neck of both males and females, but they are largest on males.

Turkey Pardoning

Every year, before Thanksgiving, a ceremony is held at the White House, in Washington D.C., during which the president "pardons" a domestic turkey, so it can live out its full natural life. Traditionally the turkey comes from the home state of the chairman of the National Turkey Federation.

A large flap of skin called a wattle hangs under the male wild turkey's chin.

The breed of turkey chosen for the ceremony is usually the broad–breasted white. Usually, it is male, chosen for its appearance and its gobbling sounds.

115

Game Birds

"Game birds" is the description for a range of wild landfowl that have often been hunted by humans for their meat. They have fleshy bodies, short wings, and strong legs. None of them is flightless, but few of them fly far, so only a handful of species make a yearly migration.

Grouse on the Ground

There are about 20 species of grouse, which live in the northern hemisphere, from temperate regions to the edge of the Arctic. To keep warm in winter, grouse have feathered legs. They feed on leaves, twigs, and buds close to the ground, also eating grit to break up this tough plant material in their gizzard. Grouse have strong feet, which they use to scrape a nest hollow in the ground, hidden by nearby plants.

The wattles of this Alaskan willow ptarmigan have flushed bright red to attract a female.

A male greater sage grouse displays his plumage, inflating the two yellow sacs on either side of his neck. This grouse eats sagebrush plants in the shrubland of western North America.

The Alaskan willow ptarmigan, also known as the willow grouse, feeds on willows, eating leaves in summer, twigs in winter, and buds in spring.

SWAINSON'S FRANCOLIN

Length: 13 to 15 in (33 to 38 cm)

Range: Southern Africa

Habitat: Grassland and shrubland

Diet: Roots, seeds, berries, grass, insects, and spiders

Conservation: Not at risk

Swainson's francolin

Social Quails

Quails are small and sociable birds, often gathering in flocks called coveys, bevies, or queers. If threatened by a predator, most quail run and hide in undergrowth rather than take flight. They are known for their distinctive calls, from the crackling "Wet my lips" of the male common quail to the insect-like buzzing of the Montezuma quail.

The male California quail has a curving black crest of six feathers. The female's crest is brown.

This male is in his breeding plumage for the spring mating season. In summer, he will be completely brown, then turn entirely white in winter for camouflage against the snow.

DID YOU KNOW? Common quail sometimes feed on poisonous plants, resulting in no ill-effects for them but an illness called coturnism in the humans that eat them.

Pheasants

These large, long-tailed gamebirds are native to Asia. The most widespread species is the common pheasant, which was transported across the world to be kept on farms or hunted for its meat. Today, it lives wild in Asia, Europe, North America, Australia, and New Zealand.

Learning to Fear Humans

As soon as a flock of common pheasants has been hunted by humans, the birds link the sound of humans with danger. Pheasants have excellent hearing and also use their feet to feel the vibrations made by footsteps. As hunters approach, the flock hides among long grasses and shrubs. Hunters often use gun dogs, such as retrievers, to "flush" the birds from their hiding places. The birds burst into flight at up to 56 mph (90 km/h), giving a "Kok kok kok" alarm call.

This male common pheasant has a blue–green head, red wattle, and white neck ring.

BLOOD PHEASANT

Length: 15 to 19 in (39 to 48 cm)

Range: Himalayan Mountains, in Asia

Habitat: Mountain forest and shrubland

Diet: Moss, leaves, grass, and insects

Conservation: Population slowly shrinking

A male blood pheasant

DID YOU KNOW? The Romans introduced common pheasants to much of their European empire around 2,000 years ago.

Sexual Dimorphism

All of the 40 species of pheasants are very sexually dimorphic, which means that males and females look different from each other. Males are larger than females, have longer tails, are brightly colored, and are decorated with wattles or crests. Females are usually well camouflaged, with mottled brown plumage.

Hoping to attract a nearby female, a male Lady Amherst's pheasant displays his plumage, raising his beautifully patterned neck ruff.

FEMALE

MALE

These two males are displaying their plumage on a good perch, spreading their bright orange neck ruffs.

The male's tail is up to 28 in (70 cm) long, twice the length of his body.

Peafowl

There are three species of peafowl: the Indian peafowl, the green peafowl of Southeast Asia, and the Congo peafowl of central Africa. Male peafowls, which are called peacocks, are best known for their courtship display, when they fan their long "train."

The Indian peacock's fan-shaped crest is made of feathers with bare shafts and blue-green, webbed tips.

Indian Peafowl

The Indian peafowl is native to the forests of South Asia, but was introduced around the world by humans in awe of the male's beauty (pictured right). Indian peafowl wander the ground in small groups, looking for berries, grains, and small animals such as lizards. When startled, they give loud and piercing "Pia-ow" calls. Peafowl run from predators, but do fly into trees to roost.

When attracting a mate, the peacock fans open the 200 feathers of his train, which are up to 5 ft (1.5 m) long. These feathers are uppertail coverts, which grow from his back and cover his much shorter tail.

The female Indian peafowl, known as a peahen, is well camouflaged, with the only brightness her iridescent green neck and breast. Both male and female chicks are mottled brown.

A Congo peacock

CONGO PEAFOWL

Length: 24 to 27.5 in (60 to 70 cm)

Range: Democratic Republic of the Congo, in Africa

Habitat: Rainforest

Diet: Fruit and insects

Conservation: Population shrinking due to habitat loss

DID YOU KNOW? Indian peahens prefer to mate with the males with the most eyecatching tails, probably because extra-luxurious tails are a sign of healthiness.

Most train feathers end in an "eyespot," its plume reflecting the sunlight in glittering blues and greens.

Green Peafowl

Unlike Indian peafowl, green peacocks and peahens look quite similar to each other, except in the mating season, when the feathers of the male's uppertail coverts grow up to 5.2 ft (1.6 m) long. The peacock fans and quivers this train, to make the colorful eyespots more dazzling. After mating, the peacock molts these ungainly feathers.

A green peacock roosts high in a forest tree, while his mate takes flight.

Lyrebirds

Lyrebirds are among the few passerines (see page 67) that spend most of their time on the ground. These unusual, forest-dwelling Australian birds have few close relatives. Lyrebirds evolved a long time ago, with fossils of birds very similar to modern lyrebirds dating back 15 million years.

Lyre-Shaped Tails

There are two species of lyrebirds, the superb lyrebird and Albert's lyrebird. Unlike most passerines, which have 12 tail feathers, lyrebirds have 16. The tails of adult males have one pair of ribbon-like feathers, six pairs of pale lace-like feathers, and an outer pair of large, curving feathers that form the shape of a lyre, an ancient stringed instrument. The tails of females and chicks are brown for camouflage on the forest floor.

A male superb lyrebird fans his tail during a courtship display, tipping it right forward over his head.

The female superb lyrebird will lay just one egg in her nest. The brown-gray, blotchy egg is well camouflaged.

LYREBIRD NEST

Messy Nests

The female builds her nest alone, positioning it on the forest floor, often among rocks or even in a cave. She spends around three weeks collecting sticks, leaves, bark, and moss, which she arranges in a dome shape, with a side entrance. The finished nest looks almost like a pile of fallen leaves and branches, which makes it hard for predators to spot.

ALBERT'S LYREBIRD

Length: 28 to 35 in (70 to 90 cm)

Range: Southeastern Queensland and northeastern New South Wales, in Australia

Habitat: Rainforest and montane forest

Diet: Insects and other small invertebrates

Conservation: Population shrinking due to habitat loss, hunting by introduced species, and forest fires

Albert's lyrebird

Lyrebirds are excellent mimics, copying the sounds of up to 20 species of other birds' songs as well as chainsaws, workmen, and computer games.

The superb lyrebird feeds on insects, spiders, and worms it finds beneath leaves on the forest floor or in rotting logs.

The superb lyrebird's throat is red-brown, while the head and back are gray to brown.

DID YOU KNOW? The male superb lyrebird's tail feathers are pictured on the reverse of the Australian 10 cent coin.

Megapodes

In ancient Greek, megapode means "huge foot." This family of mostly Australasian birds are named for their large, sharp-clawed feet and strong legs, which they use to build mounds in which they bury their eggs to keep them warm until hatching.

Mound Builders

Most birds use their body heat to incubate their eggs, but the 21 species of megapodes use heat from the ground. Male malleefowl and brushturkeys scrape together giant mounds of decaying leaves, bark, and twigs. As the plant material rots, it gives off heat. The maleo and Tongan megapode bury their eggs in sand warmed by the sun's heat or by underground volcanic activity.

A powerful male builds a nest of plant material for several local females. He uses his beak to check the temperature inside the mound.

The male malleefowl (front) builds a mound up to 2 ft (60 cm) high, which he mixes after rainfall to encourage the material to decay. After the female (back) lays her eggs, the male adds or removes material to keep the temperature right.

Length: 22 to 24 in (55 to 60 cm)

Range: Island of Sulawesi, in Indonesia, Southeast Asia

Habitat: Rainforest; nests in open sandy areas, beaches, and volcanic soils

Diet: Fruit, seeds, insects, and other small invertebrates

Conservation: Population shrinking due to habitat loss and stealing of eggs by humans

MALEO

A nesting maleo

The male Australian brushturkey's red head becomes very bright during the mating season.

Super Chicks

Megapode parents do not look after their chicks. In order to survive, the chicks are born fully feathered and are able to fly and find food within a day. Unlike other chicks, megapodes do not have an egg tooth (see page 61): they use their strong claws to break open their egg and force their way out of the mound.

A maleo chick has wriggled and clawed itself to the surface. In a moment, it will run into the nearby rainforest to hide.

Despite its wattle, the Australian brushturkey is not closely related to true turkeys.

DID YOU KNOW? Although maleos are about the size of a chicken, their eggs are five times bigger, because maleo chicks are so well developed.

Glossary

ADAPTATION
A characteristic of an animal that makes it suited to its habitat and lifestyle.

AMPHIBIAN
An animal that lives both on land and in water, such as a frog.

BARB
A strong branch extending from the central stalk of a feather.

CAMOUFLAGE
The way the color and shape of an animal make it less visible in its habitat.

CAPTIVE BREEDING
Keeping animals in a zoo or other safe place, where they can mate and increase in number.

CLASS
A scientific group that includes animals with the same body plan, such as birds or mammals.

CLIMATE CHANGE
Rising global temperatures and changes in weather patterns caused mainly by human activities.

CLUTCH
A group of eggs laid at the same time.

COLONY
A group of birds living together.

CONSERVATION
Protecting animals and plants from damage by human activity.

CONTOUR FEATHER
One of a bird's outer feathers, which form its smooth outline and help with flight.

COURTSHIP
Behavior that aims to attract a mate.

COVERT
A feather that covers the base of a main wing or tail feather.

CROP
A pouch in a bird's foodpipe.

DINOSAUR
An animal belonging to an extinct group of reptiles, related to birds.

DOMESTIC
Tame and kept by humans.

DOWN FEATHER
A small, soft, warm feather that is found below an adult bird's contour feathers.

EVOLVE
To change gradually over time.

FACIAL DISK
Bowl-shaped patterns of feathers around the eyes of some birds.

FLEDGE
To develop wing feathers that are large enough for flight.

FRESHWATER
Unsalted water, such as rivers, lakes, and ponds.

GENUS
A scientific group that includes species that are very similar to each other.

GIZZARD
A muscly part of a bird's stomach that grinds food, often using swallowed grit.

GLAND
An organ in the body that makes a substance for use in the body or for release.

GLIDING
Flying through the air without flapping the wings.

HABITAT
The natural home or environment of an animal or plant.

HEMISPHERE
Half of the planet, such as the northern or southern half on either side of the equator.

INCUBATION
The period when eggs must be kept at the right temperature before hatching.

INVASIVE
Describes an animal or other living thing that has arrived in a new place and has a harmful effect.

INVERTEBRATE
An animal without a backbone, such as an insect, spider, crab, or squid.

IRIDESCENT
Shining with bright colors that seem to change with movement.

LANDFOWL
A group of heavy-bodied birds that feed on the ground, including chickens, turkeys, grouse, and quail.

LENGTH
The measurement between the tip of a bird's beak and the tip of the tail.

MAMMAL
An animal with hair or fur that feeds its young on milk, such as a human or dog.

MANDIBLE
The upper or lower part of a bird's beak.

MIGRATE
To move from one region to another at particular times of year.

MOLLUSK
An invertebrate with a soft body and sometimes a hard shell, such as a slug, snail, clam, or octopus.

MUDFLAT
Muddy land that is left uncovered when the sea draws out at low tide.

NECTAR
A sugary liquid made by flowers.

NOCTURNAL
Active at night.

PARASITE
A living thing that lives in, on, or around another living thing, taking food and other benefits from it.

PASSERINE
A bird with three toes pointing forward and a fourth toe pointing backward, which enables it to perch on branches.

PLUMAGE
A bird's covering of feathers.

POLYGAMOUS
Having more than one mate in the same season.

PREDATOR
An animal that hunts other animals.

PREENING
Tidying and cleaning the feathers, usually with the beak.

PREY
An animal that is killed by another animal for food.

PRIMARY FEATHERS
The long feathers on the outer wing, which are used for flight.

RANGE
The area where an animal is found.

RATITE
A bird with small or basic wings and a differently shaped breastbone, which makes it unable to fly.

REGURGITATE
To bring swallowed food back up into the mouth.

REMIGES
The long feathers in the wings, which are important for flight.

REPTILE
An animal with a dry, scaly skin that lays eggs on land, such as a lizard.

RETRICES
The long feathers in the tail, which are important for flight.

ROOST
To settle down to rest or sleep, sometimes in a large group.

SCAVENGER
An animal that feeds on dead animals that it has not killed itself.

SEXUAL DIMORPHISM
Obvious differences in size or appearance between the males and females in a species.

SHRUBLAND
An area where most plants are shrubs or bushes.

SOARING
Flying without flapping the wings, while riding on rising warm air.

SPECIES
A group of living things with similar characteristics that can mate with each other.

STREAMLINED
Shaped so that air, or water, passes easily around, enabling fast travel.

SUBTROPICAL
In the areas to the south or north of the tropics, with very hot weather for some of the year.

TALONS
Strong, hooked claws.

TEMPERATE
In the areas between the subtropics and polar regions, where it is neither very hot nor very cold.

TERRITORY
An area defended by a bird or group of birds against others of the same species or sex.

TROPICAL
In the area around the equator, where it is very hot all year.

WEBBED FEET
Having toes that are linked by tissue and skin, making them paddle-like for swimming.

WETLAND
Land such as swamps and marshes, which is covered by water either throughout the year or during particular seasons.

WINGSPAN
The distance across the wings, measured from wingtip to wingtip.

ZYGODACTYL
Having two toes pointing forward and two backward.

Index

128